What SUCCESSFUL
Math Teachers Do,
Grades PreK-5

What SUCCESSFUL Math Teachers Do, Grades PreK-5

 Research-Based Strategies for the Standards-Based Classroom

Edward S. Wall ● Alfred S. Posamentier

 CORWIN PRESS
A SAGE Publications Company
Thousand Oaks, California

For information:

Corwin Press
A Sage Publications Company
2455 Teller Road
Thousand Oaks, California 91320
www.corwinpress.com

Sage Publications Ltd.
1 Oliver's Yard
55 City Road
London EC1Y 1SP
United Kingdom

Sage Publications India Pvt. Ltd.
B-42, Panchsheel Enclave
Post Box 4109
New Delhi 110 017 India

Printed in the United States of America

Library of Congress Cataloging-in-Publication Data

Wall, Edward S.
What successful math teachers do, grades preK–5: 47 research-based strategies for the standards-based classroom / Edward S. Wall, Alfred S. Posamentier.
    p. cm.
Includes bibliographical references and index.
ISBN 1-4129-1502-3; 978-1-4129-1502-1 (cloth : acid-free paper) — ISBN 1-4129-1503-1; 978-1-4129-1503-8 (pbk. : acid-free paper)
    1. Mathematics—Study and teaching (Primary)—Standards—United States.
I. Posamentier, Alfred S. II. Title.
QA13.W345 2007
372.7—dc22

                                                                    2006009057

BK
$ 24.88

This book is printed on acid-free paper.

06   07   08   09   10   10   9   8   7   6   5   4   3   2   1

Acquisitions Editor:	Faye Zucker
Editorial Assistant:	Gem Rabanera
Production Editor:	Melanie Birdsall
Typesetter:	C&M Digitals (P) Ltd.
Copy Editor:	Cheryl Rivard
Indexer:	Naomi Linzer
Cover Designer:	Michael Dubowe
Graphic Designer:	Audrey Snodgrass

Contents

Prologue

Effective mathematics teaching has, as its beginning, thoughtful preparation and, as its end, student mastery of the mathematics content. In the moment of instruction, such teaching requires that a teacher, taking into account the current mathematics development of her students, actively transform her plans and goals into student learning of substantial mathematics. However, there is nothing more difficult than imagining how such teacher actions might best be accomplished without seeing it being demonstrated. The purpose of this book is to give the reader a glimpse—through vignettes, abbreviated stories of teaching and learning, featuring the work of exemplary elementary mathematics teachers—of the research-based strategies successful elementary mathematics teachers use when they teach in a manner that is consistent with those teaching practices and learning experiences recommended by the National Council of Teachers of Mathematics (NCTM) in their *Principles and Standards for School Mathematics (PSSM).*[1]

Such teaching can be challenging work. The NCTM recommends teaching that, taking into account children's mathematical development, encourages mathematical questions, conjectures, and explanations; ensures procedural competency; and develops deep mathematical understandings. However, many elementary teachers and elementary teacher candidates have not experienced such teaching or learning. This, as the following vignette[2] illustrates, may cause a cognitive disjunction[3] when teachers are called upon by their school district to teach a curriculum that requires many of the teaching practices and incorporates many of the learning experiences suggested by the *PSSM:*

> Two third-grade teachers, Ms. Kim and Mr. Jackson, are in their first months of using a new mathematics textbook that incorporates many of the suggestions of the *PSSM.* For example, the lessons set forth have the potential to encourage students to make sense of, construct, and compute their own addition problems and, furthermore, have the potential to intellectually engage students in mathematics problem solving.

One morning Ms. Kim is working on a coin problem from the new textbook with her class. Ms. Kim asks the class, "I have pennies, nickels, and dimes in my pocket. Suppose that I pull out three coins. How much money might I have?" One boy shouts out, "That's easy. Three cents!" "Good, Raymond," says Ms. Kim, "although I don't want people to shout out answers. Now, put that in your notebook, and then think: What other solutions can you find?" The children set to work, finding solutions. After about 20 minutes, Ms. Kim calls the class together and conducts a discussion of the problem. She records the different solutions that the students propose in a chart, ordered from the least amount to the most, at the same time modeling the invention of notation (ppn for penny, penny, penny; pnn for penny, nickel, nickel; etc.) to organize and record the different coin combinations for each amount.

A few days later, Mr. Jackson is on the same lesson. He assigns the same problem and gets, as the text suggests, his students working independently. A few students ask how many coins were in the person's pocket. Mr. Jackson peers at the text. "I guess they don't tell you," he remarks. Several ask him for help, and he carefully shows them that they can combine coins to see what the amount is. "There are a few different answers," he tells his class, "so everyone should have, at least, two." As the children finish, they turn in their papers. He glances at several. They have answers written on them—different amounts of money on some, combinations of coins on others. He hands back a paper that has only one answer. "I told you two," he says to Danny. He stacks a practice addition worksheet next to the finished workbasket so that the students who finish more quickly will have something to do.

Ms. Kim chooses to conduct her lesson in a manner similar to that recommend by *PSSM*. Mr. Jackson, it appears, chooses to do the lesson in a different manner. This does not mean that Mr. Jackson lacks mathematics content knowledge or pedagogical skills. However, as with many preK–5 teachers we have mentored and taught, Mr. Jackson may not have had some of the relevant experiences that would prepare him to effectively teach a lesson of this sort.

We have found, in our own teaching and mentoring, that there are a number of learning experiences that might prepare teachers and teacher candidates to realize the suggestions of the *PSSM* in actual classroom practice. For example, there is a deepening engagement in the mathematics of preK–5; observation in exemplary preK–5 mathematics classrooms and video of such classrooms; and discussion of relevant case studies and education research. However, while observation of the teaching of mathematics often has one of the most significant impacts on teaching dispositions, there are often a limited number of preK–5 classrooms in any school or district that might be considered appropriate exemplars of the NCTM Standards. In such instances, the thoughtful analysis of mathematics vignettes—that is, short reinterpretations of actual mathematics teaching and learning in the classroom—can provide a useful supplement.

One of the first collections of such vignettes was the Professional Standards for Teaching Mathematics[4]; however, the intervening years have seen a number of other collections, of which the *PSSM* is perhaps the most well known. A primary goal in writing this book was to consolidate certain collections to further illustrate how a teacher might teach a preK–5 mathematics that exemplifies teaching practices that accord with the NCTM Standards. The book is designed to be an easy and ready reference for the preK–5 mathematics teacher. It consists of ten chapters that mirror much of the content and structure of the *PSSM*. Each chapter presents a collection of teaching strategies organized into subchapters by grade bands—Grades PreK–2 and Grades 3–5—concisely presented in a friendly format:

Grade-Band Introduction

We begin each grade-band section with a short discussion of the chapter topic for that grade band. For example, we begin the preK- through second-grade band of the chapter titled "Reasoning and Proof" by noting that students need to be encouraged by teachers to make sense of mathematics and to be guided by teachers to test whether their mathematical generalizations are correct. We begin the third- through fifth-grade band of that chapter with a short discussion of students' prior understandings of proof and how teachers might use these understandings to guide students in the construction of acceptable forms of mathematical explanation.

Strategy

We give a simple and crisp statement of the teaching strategy being recommended.

NCTM Standard

We give an exact statement of the relevant NCTM Standard.

What Research and the NCTM Standards Say

We give, in most cases, a brief restatement of what the *PSSM* says about a particular NCTM Standard together with references to relevant research. This section is intended to simply give the teacher some confidence in, and a deeper understanding of, the particular teaching strategy being addressed.

Classroom Application

We present a vignette chosen to exemplify the recommended teaching strategy. These vignettes come from a variety of sources: NCTM publications (most particularly the *PSSM*), accounts of mathematics research, units for mathematics instruction, and published observations of mathematics classrooms. In many cases these vignettes are adaptations of the original source material (moderate adaptations are usually marked by pseudonyms that differ from those originally used). The vignettes necessarily lack much of their original context—planning, resources, layout of the classroom, and follow-up are, most usually, not depicted—and have been purposively refocused on the teaching strategy. However, every effort has been taken to preserve the substance of mathematics done by teacher and students and the character of student explanations and discussions.

Although the majority of the vignettes are set in classrooms, the first vignettes of the chapters on Numbers and Operations and Algebra purposefully feature the preschool child and purposefully are set in the home. There are two primary reasons for this choice. First, a young child's early experiences of mathematics significantly influence his or her later engagement with mathematics in the primary grades.[5] Interactions with peers, siblings, and caregivers are especially formative. Primary teachers need to be aware of the possibility of such experiences as they can use these for further in-school mathematics instruction and as a means of reinforcing and validating current and later mathematical experiences in the child's larger world.

Second, the mathematics that a preschool child needs to master can often be taken for granted by caregivers and teachers (including preK teachers). It is no minor task for a child to realize that the squiggle 9 somehow comes right after the squiggle 8 or to realize that there might be some benefit to arranging objects neatly so that they may be purposively counted. Further, it is important to realize that in the early years, such notions as cardinality—the notion that, beginning with one, the last sequential number tagged might be the total number of objects in a set—are often far from obvious.

Precautions and Possible Pitfalls

 We specify, for each vignette, some of the possible pitfalls that need to be taken into consideration when implementing or extending that teaching strategy.

Sources

We provide references to relevant research and curriculum implementations so that readers can further investigate reasons for, and implementations of, a particular standard or strategy. Many of these references come from the *PSSM*. Where we felt these might not be sufficient, we have provided references from recent mathematics education research. We note that many of these later references are to articles in *A Research Companion to Principles and Standards for School Mathematics,*[6] which was explicitly written to accompany the *PSSM*.

As you read through the vignettes offered in this book, we hope you will thoughtfully reflect on the mathematics featured, the explanations and comments of the students, and the manner in which a teacher implements a particular strategy. We recommend, for example, that you do the featured mathematics. Mathematics is not a spectator sport—especially that of young children. You may also wish to compare what you read with your own experiences as a mathematics learner and as a mathematics teacher. Think about what you found then, or now see, as difficult, and remember that much of the mathematics that now seems obvious to you was, most likely, somewhat challenging in your elementary school years. Above all, note that "Excellence in mathematics education requires equity—high expectations and strong support of all students."[7]

Notes

1. NCTM. (2000). *Principles and standards for school mathematics.* Reston, VA: NCTM.
2. Slightly adapted from Cohen, D. K., & Ball, D. L. (2001). Making change: Instruction and its improvement. *Phi Delta Kappan, 83,* 73–74.
3. See, for example, Feiman-Nemser, S., & Remillard, J. (1995). *Perspectives on learning to teach.* East Lansing, MI: Michigan State University.
4. NCTM. (1991). *Professional standards for teaching mathematics.* Reston, VA: NCTM.
5. NCES. (2000). *The kindergarten year.* Washington, DC. [On-line]. Available: http://nces.ed.gov
6. Kilpatrick, J., Martin, W. G., & Shifter, D. (Eds). (2003). *A research companion to* Principles and standards for school mathematics. Reston, VA: NCTM.
7. NCTM. (2000). *Principles and standards for school mathematics.* Reston, VA: NCTM.

Acknowledgments

Corwin Press thanks the following reviewers for their contributions to this book:

Carol Amos, Teacher Leader/Mathematics Coordinator, Twinfield Union School, Plainfield, VT

Anne Giddings, Assistant Superintendent, Ansonia Board of Education, Ansonia, CT

Trish Guinee, Mathematics Coordinator, Peoria Public Schools, Peoria, IL

Rhonda Naylor, Math Teacher/Coordinator, Campus Middle School, Englewood, CO

Allen Stevens, Math/Science Teacher, Mooresville Middle School, Mooresville, NC

About the Authors

Edward S. Wall is Assistant Professor of Elementary Mathematics Education at The City College of the City University of New York. In 1968 he received his MA in Mathematics at the University of Maryland, and after a number of years working as an applied mathematician, he received a Sloan Foundation Fellowship for the purposes of pursuing a PhD in Mathematical Biology at the University of Chicago. Along the way, he became intrigued by the very notion of teaching mathematics and, after several years, found himself deeply involved in full-time K–12 mathematics teaching. Time passed, and in 2003, he received a PhD in Mathematics Education at the University of Michigan and subsequently joined the faculty at The City College. He still finds himself intrigued by the very notion of teaching mathematics, and his research is reflective of that fascination.

Alfred S. Posamentier is Dean of the School of Education and Professor of Mathematics Education of The City College of the City University of New York. He is the author and coauthor of more than 35 mathematics books for teachers, secondary school students, and the general readership. Dr. Posamentier is also a frequent commentator in newspapers on topics relating to education.

After completing his AB degree in mathematics at Hunter College of the City University of New York, he took a position as a teacher of mathematics at Theodore Roosevelt High School in the Bronx (New York), where he focused his attention on improving the students' problem-solving skills and at the same time enriching their instruction far beyond what the traditional textbooks offered. He also developed the school's first mathematics teams (at both the junior and senior levels). He is currently involved in working with mathematics teachers, nationally and internationally, to help them maximize their effectiveness.

Immediately upon joining the faculty of The City College (after having received his master's degree there), he began to develop inservice courses for secondary school mathematics teachers, including such special areas as recreational mathematics and problem solving in mathematics.

Dr. Posamentier received his PhD from Fordham University (New York) in mathematics education and has since extended his reputation in mathematics education to Europe. He has been visiting professor at several European universities in Austria, England, Germany, and Poland, most recently at the University of Vienna (Fulbright Professor in 1990) and at the Technical University of Vienna.

In 1989, he was awarded an Honorary Fellow at the South Bank University (London, England). In recognition of his outstanding teaching, The City College Alumni Association named him Educator of the Year in 1994, and New York City had the day, May 1, 1994, named in his honor by the president of the New York City Council. In 1994, he was also awarded the Grand Medal of Honor from the Federal Republic of Austria. In 1999, upon approval of Parliament, the president of the Federal Republic of Austria awarded him the title of University Professor of Austria; in 2003, he was awarded the title of Ehrenbürger (Honorary Fellow) of the Vienna University of Technology; and he was recently (June 2004) awarded the Austrian Cross of Honor for Arts and Science First Class from the president of the Federal Republic of Austria. In 2005, Dr. Posamentier was elected to the Hall of Fame of the Hunter College Alumni Association.

He has taken on numerous important leadership positions in mathematics education locally. He was a member of the New York State Education Commissioner's Blue Ribbon Panel on the Math A Regents Exams. He is on the Commissioner's Mathematics Standards Committee, which is charged with redefining the Standards for New York State, and he is on the New York City Chancellor's Math Advisory Panel.

Now in his 36th year on the faculty of The City College, he is still a leading commentator on educational issues and continues his longtime passion of seeking ways to make mathematics interesting to teachers (see *Math Wonders: To Inspire Teachers and Students*, 2003), students, and the general public—as can be seen from his latest two books, *Math Charmers: Tantalizing Tidbits for the Mind* (2003), and π, *A Biography of the World's Most Mysterious Number* (2004).

1

Numbers and Operations

Grades PreK–2

The concepts and skills related to numbers and operations are a major emphasis of mathematics instruction in prekindergarten through Grade 2. Over this span, the small child who holds up two fingers in response to the question "How many is two?" grows to become the second grader who solves sophisticated problems using multidigit computation strategies. In these years, children's understanding of numbers develops significantly. Children come to school with rich and varied informal knowledge of numbers. During the early years teachers must help students strengthen their sense of numbers, moving from the initial development of basic counting techniques to more sophisticated understandings of the size of numbers, number relationships, patterns, operations, and place value (NCTM, 2000).

 STRATEGY 1: Encourage young children's exploration and understanding of relationships among numbers.

NCTM Standard

 Understand numbers, ways of representing numbers, relationships among numbers, and number systems.

What Research and the NCTM Standards Say (NCTM, 2000)

Counting is a foundation for students' early work with numbers. Young children are motivated to count everything from the treats they eat to the stairs they climb, and through their repeated experience with the counting process, they learn many fundamental number concepts (Ginsburg, Klein, & Starkey, 1998). They can associate number words with small collections of objects and gradually learn to count and keep track of objects in larger groups. They can establish one-to-one correspondence by moving, touching, or pointing to objects as they say the number words (Baroody & Wilkins, 1999). They should learn that counting objects in a different order does not alter the result, and they may notice that the next whole number in the counting sequence is one more than the number just named. They often solve addition and subtraction problems by counting concrete objects, and many children invent problem-solving strategies based on counting strategies (Fuson, 1988).

Classroom Applications

In this vignette (adapted from Baroody & Wilkins, 1999), we listen as five-year-old Tammy is being encouraged by her father to build on her understandings of counting to compare numbers. The vignette is set in Tammy's home as much of children's early number sense comes from one-to-one interactions with caretakers and siblings. However, similar learning experiences can be provided in classrooms by kindergarten and prekindergarten teachers.

Tammy is playing the card game War with her father. War is normally a two-player game that is played by dealing out all of the cards (in this case, face cards and jokers were removed), facedown, to each of the players. Both players then, simultaneously, turn over the top card of their pile, and the player with the highest number wins both cards. If there is a tie for the highest, then both players put a second card facedown and simultaneously turn up a third card. The player with the highest number wins all the cards played in that round. If there is again a tie, this tie-breaking procedure is repeated until one player wins or one or both players run out of cards.

During the game, Tammy drew an 8 and her father drew a 6. Unsure which number was larger, Tammy said, "Wait a minute," and then got up and went to the channel selector of the TV. She looked up each number on the channel selector and concluded, "Eight is higher than six." Soon after, a 7 and an 8 came up. She again went to the channel changer to determine the larger number. Later, a 9 and an 8 came up. "Which is bigger, Daddy?" she asked. "What do you think?" her father said. Tammy returned to the channel selector and concluded, "Nine is much bigger." Several plays later, a 9 and an 8 came up again. This time Tammy counted the spades on her 9 card ("one, two, three, four, five, six, seven, eight, nine") and took the cards because nine followed eight when she counted.

Tammy has been engaged by her father in an activity that is—in her eyes—both meaningful and challenging. If teachers and parents deliberately create such opportunities and provide such tools—a clock or some sort of number line are other examples—children can learn to become quite resourceful in their mathematics solutions.

Precautions and Possible Pitfalls

Young children are often able to count accurately to reasonably large numbers. However, such counting can be more of a chanting of number words than a purposeful one-to-one correspondence with objects, and with actual objects, such children frequently overcount, exhibiting little awareness of cardinality. It is important that teachers and parents help children—by providing opportunities to count distinct objects, in a purposeful one-to-one fashion and in context—move beyond such chanting to a deeper understanding of numbers.

Sources

Baroody, A. J., & Wilkins, J. L. M. (1999). The development of informal counting, number, and arithmetic skills and concepts. In Juanita V. Copley (Ed.), *Mathematics in the early years* (pp. 48–65). Reston, VA: NCTM, 1999.

Fuson, K. C. (1988). *Children's Counting and Concepts of Numbers*. New York: Springer-Verlag.

Ginsburg, H. P., Klein, A., & Starkey, P. (1998). The development of children's mathematical thinking: Connecting research with practice. In I. E. Sigel & K. A. Renninger (Eds.), *Child Psychology in Practice* (pp. 401–476). New York: John Wiley & Sons.

NCTM. (2000). *Principles and standards for school mathematics*. Reston, VA: NCTM.

 STRATEGY 2: Encourage young children's understanding of addition and subtraction and how they relate to each other.

NCTM Standard

 Understand meanings of operations and how they relate to one another.

What Research and the NCTM Standards Say (NCTM, 2000)

As students in the lower grades work with complex tasks in a variety of contexts, they also build an understanding of operations on numbers. Appropriate contexts can arise through student-initiated activities, teacher-created stories, and in many other ways. As students explain their written work, solutions, and mental processes, teachers gain insight into their students' thinking. An understanding of addition and subtraction can, for example, be generated when young students solve "joining" and take-away problems by directly modeling the situation or by using counting strategies, such as counting on or counting back (Carpenter & Moser, 1984). Students develop further understandings of addition when they solve missing-addend problems that arise from stories or real situations. Further understandings of subtraction are conveyed by situations in which two collections need to be made equal or one collection needs to be made a desired size. Some problems, such as "Carlos had three cookies. María gave him some more, and now he has eight. How many did she give him?" can help students see the relationship between addition and subtraction.

Classroom Applications

In this vignette (adapted from Barnett-Clarke, Ramirez, Coggins, & Alldredge, 2003, Case 1), we listen as Ms. Santi's second graders are being encouraged to deepen their understandings of subtraction.

Ms. Santi's students had been, in prior weeks, practicing addition and subtraction fact families and working on problem-solving skills involving both addition and subtraction. While Ms. Santi was out of school for a few days, the substitute teacher had taught her students to subtract when the problem asked, "How many more?" When Ms. Santi returns to school, she decides to check her students' understanding of this problem type and poses the following problem:

> Robert had 14 lollipops. Jeffrey had only 6 lollipops. How many more lollipops did Robert have?

The students quickly get to work, using a variety of manipulatives to solve the problem. While they work, Ms. Santi walks around the room and talks with them about their strategies. To her amazement, many of her students have immediately added the numbers and have 20 as their answer. Then Robert speaks up. "I drew all the lollipops too, but I only counted eight. I know the answer is eight." His work, however, shows a row of 6 lollipops at the top and 14 more scattered below. Melissa notes she got 8 too. "I made the numbers with color tiles, and I put them beside each other, and I didn't count the ones that match. I counted eight." Lourdes, looking on, insists, "You have to count all of them, because you have more than eight." At this point, most of the class begins to discuss whether you need to count all the lollipops or just some of them. Then Corey shouts excitedly, "I know how to show it! I made it with snap cubes, and I know it's eight because you put Brandon's and Jeffrey's side by side and you just count the extras!" Corey holds up his snap-cube graph for the class to see.

Figure 1.1

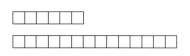

Immediate comprehension sweeps the room and several students repeat, "You just count the extras."

Trying to help her students make a connection with the previous text-book subtraction problem, Ms. Santi then asks if they thought subtraction could solve the lollipop problem. No one replies. She then asks them about the textbook subtraction problems they had completed successfully the week before. Marjorie says, "The teacher said we were to subtract on those problems." The other students quickly agree. Ms. Santi writes

$$\begin{array}{r} 14 \\ -6 \\ \hline 8 \end{array}$$

on the board and asks the students how this differs from Corey's snap-cube solution. Lourdes says, "The numbers are the same, but you have a minus sign." There is silence and then Robert raises his hand. "When you take-away, aren't you matching the six with the six in the fourteen? Then the eight are just the extras."

There is a substantial difference between knowing how to do a mathematics procedure and knowing when to do a mathematics procedure. To further develop her students' understanding of the meanings of addition and subtraction, Ms. Santi has provided a problem context that encourages them to make sense of their use of mathematics.

Precautions and Possible Pitfalls

 It is not uncommon for children, if given the opportunity to make sense of the mathematics they are doing, to solve the problem Ms. Santi posed by counting on—that is, beginning with six objects and counting eight more to make fourteen—or, as Corey said, by "counting the extras." However, many teachers—due to their own prior mathematics experiences—tend to ignore the "more" in the problem and obtain a solution through subtraction. Teachers need to build on students' mathematics intuitions by carefully bridging these solution techniques. While Corey's solution is a practical technique for small differences, subtraction, if properly understood, may be more practical for comparison of larger numbers.

Sources

Barnett-Clarke, C., Ramirez, A., Coggins, D., & Alldredge, S. (2003). *Number sense and operations in the primary grades.* Portsmouth, NH: Heinemann.

Carpenter, T. P., & Moser, J. M. (1984). The acquisition of addition and subtraction concepts in grades one through three. *Journal for Research in Mathematics Education, 15,* 179–202.

NCTM. (2000). *Principles and standards for school mathematics.* Reston, VA: NCTM.

STRATEGY 3: Encourage young children's fluent computation.

NCTM Standard

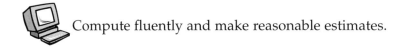 Compute fluently and make reasonable estimates.

What Research and the NCTM Standards Say (NCTM, 2000)

Young children often initially compute by using objects and counting. However, prekindergarten through Grade 2 teachers need to encourage them to shift, over time, to solving many computation problems mentally or with paper and pencil so as to record their thinking. Students should develop strategies for knowing basic number combinations (the single-digit addition pairs and their counterparts for subtraction) that build on their thinking about, and understanding of, numbers. Fluency—that is, students are able to compute efficiently and accurately with single-digit numbers—with basic addition and subtraction number combinations is a goal for the preK–2 years.

As students work with larger numbers, their strategies for computing play an important role in linking less formal knowledge with more sophisticated mathematical thinking. Research provides evidence that students will rely on their own computational strategies (Carpenter, Franke, Jacobs, Fennema, & Empson, 1998). Such inventions contribute to their mathematical development (Gravemeijer & Eskelhoff 1994; Steffe 1994).

Classroom Applications

In this vignette (adapted from NCTM, 2000, pp. 86–87), we listen as Mr. Daley's second graders are being encouraged, building on classroom discussions of addition, to model and record their addition strategies.

Mr. Daley has posed the following addition problem to his class of second graders:

> We have 153 students at our school. There are 273 students at the school down the street. How many students are in both schools?

While his students work, he walks around the room observing and listening to their strategies. His students give a variety of responses that illustrate a range of understandings. For example, Raul models the problem with bean sticks that the class has made earlier in the year, using hundreds rafts, tens sticks, and loose beans. He then draws a picture of his model and labels the parts, "3 rafts," "12 tens," "6 beans."

Ana first adds the hundreds and records 300 as an intermediate result. She then adds the tens, and, keeping the answer in her head, adds the ones. Finally, she adds the partial results—300 + 12 tens + 6—and writes down 426 as the answer. Other students use the conventional algorithm (stacking the addends and then adding the ones, adding the tens and renaming them as hundreds and tens, and finally adding the hundreds). Most do this accurately, but some write 3126 as their answer. Stacy finds the answer using mental computation and writes nothing down except her answer. When Mr. Daly asks her to explain, she says, "Well, two hundreds and one hundred are three hundreds, and five tens and five tens are ten tens, or another hundred, so that's four hundreds. There's still two tens left over, and three and three is six, so it's four hundred and twenty-six."

Problems such as the one posed by Mr. Daley give his students meaningful opportunities to reflect on and fluently apply their knowledge of numbers and operations. Simultaneously, he gains deeper insights into his students' misconceptions and mistakes and thus is better able to design, if necessary, further and relevant practice. Later in the lesson, Mr. Daley will ask his students to explain their strategies to their classmates. Such presentations can provide further opportunities for practice, application, and reflection.

Precautions and Possible Pitfalls

Properly understood, facility in computation is neither purely a product of practice nor purely a product of understanding growing, as it does, out of their interplay. By allowing students to work in ways that have meaning for them and by encouraging them to develop efficient strategies, teachers can gain insight—through student explanations—into students' developing understanding and give them guidance. Such meaningful practice, rather than only drilling isolated number facts, is necessary to develop fluency with basic number combinations and strategies with multidigit numbers.

Sources

Carpenter, T. P., Franke, M. L., Jacobs, V. R., Fennema, E., & Empson, S. B. (1998). A longitudinal study of invention and understanding in children's multidigit addition and subtraction. *Journal for Research in Mathematics Education, 29,* 3–20.

Gravemeijer, K., & Eskelhoff, P. (1994). *Developing Realistic Mathematics Instruction.* Utrecht, Netherlands: Freudenthal Institute.

NCTM. (2000). *Principles and standards for school mathematics.* Reston, VA: NCTM.

Steffe, L. P. (1994). Children's multiplying schemes. In G. Harel & J. Confrey (Eds.), *The development of multiplicative reasoning in the learning of mathematics* (pp. 3–39). Albany: State University of New York Press.

Grades 3–5

Most students enter Grade 3 with enthusiasm for, and interest in, learning mathematics. In fact, nearly three-quarters of U.S. fourth graders report liking mathematics (Silver, Strutchens, & Zawojewski, 1997). They find it practical and believe that what they are learning is important. If the mathematics studied in Grades 3–5 is interesting and understandable, the increasingly sophisticated mathematical ideas at this level can maintain students' engagement and enthusiasm. But if their learning becomes a process of simply mimicking and memorizing, they can soon begin to lose interest. Instruction at this level must be active and intellectually stimulating and must help students make sense of mathematics (NCTM, 2000).

STRATEGY 4: *Encourage an understanding of the structure of numbers and relationships among numbers.*

NCTM Standard

Understand numbers, ways of representing numbers, relationships among numbers, and number systems.

What Research and the NCTM Standards Say (NCTM, 2000)

In Grades 3–5, students' study and use of numbers should be extended to include larger numbers, fractions, and decimals. They need to develop strategies for judging the relative sizes of numbers. They should understand more deeply the multiplicative nature of the number system, including the structure of 786 as 700 plus 80 plus 6. Students who understand the structure of numbers and the relationships among numbers can work with them flexibly. They recognize and can generate equivalent representations for the same number. For example, 36 can be thought of as $30 + 6$, $20 + 16$, 9×4, $40 - 4$, three dozen, or the square of 6. Each form is useful for a particular situation. Thinking of 36 as $30 + 6$ may be useful when multiplying by 36, whereas thinking of it as 6 sixes or 4 nines is helpful when considering equal shares. Students who understand the structure of numbers and the relationships among numbers can work with them more flexibly (Fuson, 1992). Students need to have many experiences decomposing and composing numbers in order to develop such understanding.

Classroom Applications

In this vignette (adapted from Fosnot & Dolk, 2001, p. 45), we listen as Ms. Freeman's third graders study, within a particular context, the associative and commutative properties of multiplication.

Ms. Freeman has asked her students to investigate how many different-sized boxes they can make that would hold 36 chocolates (for example, a box of $2 \times 6 \times 3$ chocolates).

As Ms. Freeman walks around the room listening to her students discuss the problem, she stops at the table where Sara and Mercedes are working. Sara and Mercedes have 36 multilink cubes (each cube, measuring a cubic unit, represents a chocolate) arranged in a box with dimensions of 2 by 3 by 6. On graph paper they have drawn the base of the box as 3 by 6. Next to the drawing Mercedes has written, "(3 × 6) × 2. The bottom has 3 rows of 6. It has 2 layers."

Sara smiles at Ms. Freeman and then turns to Mercedes. "I'm confused," she explains, "I see six rows of three."

Figure 1.2

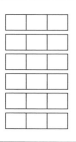

"Where?" Mercedes asks. Sara points. "See, three, six, nine, twelve, fifteen, eighteen." "Oh, yeah," Mercedes exclaims, "but see, six and six and six."

Figure 1.3

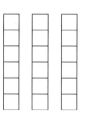

"Hey, let's write both!" They write, "(3 × 6) × 2" and "(6 × 3) × 2." Then Mercedes asks, "How else can we turn it? Oh, I know, we could make this side be the bottom!" She turns the box so that the 3-by-2 side becomes the base.

Figure 1.4

"Now we have one, two, three, four, five, six layers!" "Yeah, and we can write it two ways," Sara, looking at Ms. Freeman, proudly declares as she writes, "(2 × 3) × 6" and then "(3 × 2) × 6."

Ms. Freeman has provided a mathematics context in which her students are being encouraged to explore the various multiplicative representations of 36. Even though Sara and Mercedes are presently working with only the factors 2, 3, and 6, they are developing a practical awareness of the important mathematics principles of commutativity and associativity. Experience with these principles is essential if students are to deepen their understandings of number representations and relationships.

Precautions and Possible Pitfalls

 Manipulatives can provide opportunities for students to model and investigate significant number relationships such as the associative and commutative properties. However, manipulatives, unless purposively and deliberately utilized for the doing of important mathematics, are often ineffective in developing students' mathematical knowledge or fluency. A child playing with square blocks, for example, is unlikely to naturally realize that the cube of the length of a side is the volume. Manipulatives do not transparently embody mathematical truths (Ball, 1992).

Sources

Ball, D. L. (1992). Magical hopes: Manipulatives and the reform of math education, *American Educator*, 14–47.

Fosnot, C. T., & Dolk, D. (2001). *Young mathematicians at work: Constructing multiplication and division.* Portsmouth, NH: Heinemann.

Fuson, K. C. (1992). Research on learning and teaching addition and subtraction of whole numbers. In G. Leinhardt, R. Putnam, & R. A. Hattrup (Eds.), *Analysis of arithmetic for mathematics teaching* (pp. 53–188). Hillsdale, NJ: Lawrence Erlbaum Associates.

NCTM. (2000). *Principles and standards for school mathematics.* Reston, VA: NCTM.

Silver, E. A., Strutchens, M. E., & Zawojewski, J. S. (1997). NAEP findings regarding race/ethnicity and gender: Affective issues, mathematics performance, and instructional context. In P. A. Kenney & E. A. Silver (Eds.), *Results from the Sixth Mathematics Assessment of the National Assessment of Educational Progress* (pp. 33–59). Reston, VA: National Council of Teachers of Mathematics.

 STRATEGY 5: Encourage an understanding of the meanings of multiplication and division and how they relate to each other.

NCTM Standard

Understand meanings of operations and how they relate to one another.

What Research and the NCTM Standards Say (NCTM, 2000)

In Grades 3–5, students should focus on the meanings of, and relationship between, multiplication and division. It is important that students understand what each number in a multiplication or division expression represents. For example, in multiplication, unlike addition, the factors in the problem can refer to different units. Modeling multiplication problems with pictures, diagrams, or concrete materials helps students learn what the factors and their product represent in various contexts.

Students can extend their understanding of multiplication and division as they consider the inverse relationship between the two operations. Using models—such as multiplicative arrays (Fuson, 2003) or calculators (NCTM, 2000)—to explore the effect of multiplying or dividing numbers can also lead to a deeper understanding of these operations.

Classroom Applications

Ms. Pierce's fourth-grade class has recently completed a unit on multiplication and division. In this vignette (adapted from NCTM, 1991), we listen as Ms. Pierce introduces the topic of factors and multiples. Ms. Pierce has chosen to use the calculator as a tool in this initial lesson.

The fourth graders, using the automatic constant feature of their calculators (for example, pressing 5 + = = = . . . yields 5, 10, 15, 20 . . . on the calculator display), generate lists of the multiples of different numbers. They also use the calculator to explore the factors of different numbers. To encourage the students to deepen their understanding of the structure of numbers, Ms. Pierce urges them to look for patterns and to make conjectures by asking them, "Do you see any patterns in the lists you are making? Can you make any guesses about any of those patterns?"

Shannaz and Maria raise a question that has attracted the interest of the whole class:

Are there more multiples of 3 or more multiples of 8?

"What do the rest of you think?" Ms. Pierce asks. "How could you investigate this question? I want you to work on this a bit on your own or with a partner, and then let's discuss what you come up with."

The students pursue the question excitedly. The calculators are useful once more as students generate lists of the multiples of 3 and the multiples of 8. Groups form around particular arguments. Sinting, Sharda, and

Jonnatun argue that there are more multiples of 3 because in the interval between 0 and 20, there are more multiples of 3 than multiples of 8. Raul, Melissa, and Leigh are convinced that the multiples of 3 are "just as many as the multiples of eight because they go on forever." John and Derrick, thinking that there should be more multiples of 8 because 8 is greater than 3, form a new conjecture about numbers—that the larger the number, the more factors it has.

Ms. Pierce takes up this last conjecture and says to the class, "That's an interesting conjecture. Let's just think about it for a second. How many factors does, say, three have?" Michel replies, "One and three." "Let's try another one," continues Ms. Pierce. "What about twenty?" Natasha replies, "One and twenty, two and ten, four and five." The period is drawing to an end, and as Ms. Pierce looks up at the clock, Brody asks, "But what about seventeen? It doesn't seem to work?" Ms. Pierce smiles and replies, "That's one of the things that you could examine for tomorrow. I want all of you to see if you can find out if this conjecture always holds."

Ms. Pierce has provided a context that provides an opportunity for her students to build on their knowledge of multiplication and division in order to practice the mathematical notions of factor and multiple and to explore how they are related to each other. Explorations such as this are also important in enriching students' understanding and sense of the multiplicative structure of numbers.

Precautions and Possible Pitfalls

Students can learn mathematics more deeply with the appropriate use of technology (Groves & Stacey, 1998). Technology should not, however, be used as a replacement for basic understandings and intuitions; rather, it can and should be used to help foster those understandings and intuitions. Students at this age should begin to develop good decision-making habits about when it is useful and appropriate to use other computational methods, rather than reach for a calculator. Teachers should create opportunities for these decisions as well as make judgments about when and how calculators can be used to support learning.

Sources

Fuson, K. C. (2003). Developing mathematical power in whole number operations. In J. Kilpatrick, W. G. Martin, & D. Schifter (Eds.), *A research companion to NCTM's standards* (pp. 68–94). Reston, VA: NCTM.

Groves, S., & Stacey, K. (1998). Calculators in primary mathematics: Exploring number before teaching algorithms. In L. J. Morrow (Ed.), *The teaching and learning of algorithms in school mathematics* (pp. 120–29). Reston, VA: NCTM.

NCTM. (1991). *Professional standards for teaching mathematics.* Reston, VA: NCTM.
NCTM. (2000). *Principles and standards for school mathematics.* Reston, VA: NCTM.

 STRATEGY 6: Encourage students to compute fluently and make reasonable estimates.

NCTM Standard

Compute fluently and make reasonable estimates.

What Research and the NCTM Standards Say (NCTM, 2000)

Research suggests that by solving problems that require calculation, students develop methods for computing and also learn more about operations and properties (McClain, Cobb, & Bowers, 1998; Schifter, 1999). As students develop methods to solve multi-digit computation problems, they should be encouraged to record and share their methods. As they do so, they can learn from one another, analyze the efficiency and generalizability of various approaches, and try one another's methods. In the past, common school practice has been to present a single algorithm for each operation. However, more than one efficient and accurate computational algorithm exists for each arithmetic operation. Further, if given the opportunity, students naturally invent methods to compute that make sense to them (Fuson, 2003; Madell, 1985).

Classroom Applications

 In this vignette (adapted from NCTM, 2000, pp. 153–154), we listen as Ms. Sparks gives her fifth graders the opportunity to share their computational procedures for division.

Ms. Sparks has asked her students to share their solutions to a homework problem, 728 ÷ 34. She has asked several students to put their work on the board to be discussed, and she has deliberately chosen students who had approached the problem in several different ways. As the students put their work on the board, Ms. Sparks circulates among the other students, checking their homework.

Henry has written his solution:

$$34 \times 10 = 340$$
$$34 \times 20 = 680$$

$$
\begin{array}{rr}
680 & 728 \\
+\ 34 & -714 \\
\hline
714 & 14 \\
\end{array}
$$

Henry explains to the class, "Twenty thirty-fours plus one more is twenty-one. I knew I was pretty close. I didn't think I could add any more thirty-fours, so I subtracted seven hundred fourteen from seven hundred twenty-eight and got fourteen. Then I had twenty-one remainder fourteen." Students nod their heads in agreement.

Michaela shows her solution:

$$
\begin{array}{r}
21 \\
34\overline{)728} \\
68 \\
\hline
48 \\
34 \\
\hline
14 \\
\end{array}
$$

and says, "Thirty-four goes into seventy-two two times and that's sixty-eight. You gotta minus that, bring down the eight, then thirty-four goes into forty-eight one time." Some children do not understand Michaela's explanation, and Ms. Sparks asks if anyone can see parts of Michaela's and Henry's work that are similar.

Fashen says hesitantly, "Well, there is a six hundred eighty in Henry's and a sixty-eight in Michaela's." Ms. Sparks asks Michaela about the 68 and she replies that it is 2 times 34. Ms. Sparks says, "So, I don't get what you're saying about two times thirty-four. What does this two up here in the twenty-one represent?" Samir says, "It's twenty," and Henry remarks, "But twenty times thirty-four is six hundred eighty, not sixty-eight." Ms. Sparks writes a zero after the 68 and says, "So what if I wrote a zero here to show that this is six hundred eighty? Does that help you see any more similarities?" Maya says, "They both did twenty thirty-fours first," and Rita exclaims, "I get it. Then Michaela did, like, how many more are left, and it was forty-eight, and then she could do one more thirty-four."

Regardless of the particular algorithm used, students exhibit *computational fluency* when they are able to clearly explain their particular method, use it to compute accurately and efficiently, and recognize that other methods exist (NCTM, 2000). However, students need help in doing such work. Ms. Sparks saw important mathematics relationships between the methods described by Henry and Michaela, but she doubted that any of her students would initially see these relationships. Through deliberate questioning, she was able to help students focus on the ways in which both Michaela's and Henry's methods used multiplication to find the total number of 34s in 728 and helped students clarify what quantities were represented by the notation in Michaela's solution.

Precautions and Possible Pitfalls

Procedural and conceptual describe ways of doing mathematics and should not be used for classifying mathematics solutions. Although Michaela's solution uses the standard long division algorithm and Henry's solution seems more of his own invention (it is, in fact, common in the elementary grades), both are valid mathematics solutions. Ms. Sparks's deliberate questioning helps give Michaela's solution a conceptual basis and highlights its efficiency. However, Henry's solution can be equally or more efficient when, for example, one divides 704 by 10. For such a division, a *computationally fluent* student would not use the standard long division algorithm.

Sources

Fuson, K. C. (2003). Developing mathematical power in whole number operations. In J. Kilpatrick, W. G. Martin, & D. Schifter (Eds.), *A research companion to NCTM's standards* (pp. 68–94). Reston, VA: NCTM.

Madell, R. (1985). Children's natural processes. *Arithmetic Teacher, 32,* 20–22.

McClain, K., Cobb, P., & Bowers, J. (1998). A contextual investigation of three-digit addition and subtraction. In L. J. Morrow (Ed.), *The teaching and learning of algorithms in school mathematics* (pp. 141–150). Reston, VA: NCTM.

NCTM. (2000). *Principles and standards for school mathematics.* Reston, VA: NCTM.

Schifter, D. (1999). Reasoning about operations: Early algebraic thinking in Grades K–6. In L. V. Stiff (Ed.), *Developing mathematical reasoning in grades K–12* (pp. 62–81). Reston, VA: NCTM.

2

Algebra

Grades PreK–2

Algebraic concepts can evolve and continue to develop during prekindergarten through Grade 2. They will be manifested through work with classification, patterns and relations, operations with whole numbers, explorations of function, and step-by-step processes. Although the concepts discussed in this Standard are algebraic, this does not mean that students in the early grades are going to deal with the symbolism often taught in a traditional high school algebra course.

Even before formal schooling, children develop beginning concepts related to patterns, functions, and algebra. They learn repetitive songs, rhythmic chants, and predictive poems that are based on repeating and growing patterns. The recognition, comparison, and analysis of patterns are important components of a student's intellectual development. When students notice that operations seem to have particular properties, they are beginning to think algebraically. For example, they realize that changing the order in which two numbers are added does not change the result or that adding zero to a number leaves that number unchanged. Students' observations and discussions of how quantities relate to one another lead to initial experiences with function relationships, and their representations of mathematical situations using concrete objects, pictures, and symbols are the beginnings of mathematical modeling (NCTM, 2000).

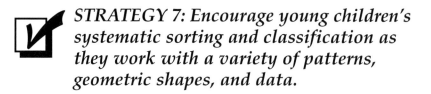

STRATEGY 7: *Encourage young children's systematic sorting and classification as they work with a variety of patterns, geometric shapes, and data.*

NCTM Standard

Understand patterns, relations, and functions.

What Research and the NCTM Standards Say (NCTM, 2000)

Sorting, classifying, and ordering facilitate children's work with patterns, geometric shapes, and data. Given a package of assorted stickers, children quickly notice many differences among the items. They can sort the stickers into groups having similar traits such as color, size, or design and order them from smallest to largest. Caregivers and teachers should elicit from children the criteria they are using as they sort and group objects. Patterns are a way for young students to recognize order and to organize their world and are important in all aspects of mathematics at this level (Clements, 2004). Preschoolers recognize patterns in their environment and through experiences in school should become more skilled in noticing patterns in arrangements of objects, shapes, and numbers and in using patterns to predict what comes next in an arrangement. Students know, for example, that "first comes breakfast, then school," and "Monday we go to art, Tuesday we go to music." Students who see the digits 0, 1, 2, 3, 4, 5, 6, 7, 8, 9 repeated over and over will see a pattern that helps them learn to count to 100—a formidable task for students who do not recognize the pattern.

Classroom Applications

In this vignette (adapted from Baroody & Wilkins, 1999), we listen as four-year-old Linda is being encouraged by her older brother, Steve, to systematically order the objects that she counts. Much of children's early algebraic thinking comes from one-to-one interactions with caretakers and siblings. Although this vignette is set in Linda's home, similar learning experiences can be provided in classrooms by kindergarten and prekindergarten teachers.

One afternoon, four-year-old Linda plays a card game with her brother and sister. When the game is over, she spreads out her cards to count how many she has won. She starts counting by pointing to each card as she says in turn, "One, two, three, four, five . . . " However, after "five," she loses track of the cards she has counted and begins to rattle off numbers as she randomly points to different cards, counting some twice.

"Linda, you're not counting right," says her six-year-old brother, Steve. "You can't just keep counting the same cards over again. It's easier if the ones you count are in a different pile," he adds. With his direction Linda moves each card she counts into a separate pile, "One, two, three, four, five, six, seven, eight, nine, ten, eleven, twelve," and concludes she has twelve.

Linda is able to count to twelve; however, her lack of experience in counting large collections of objects means that she does not yet appreciate some of the efficiencies provided by appropriate sorting, ordering, or classification. The exploration and development of a "keeping-track" strategy, such as that suggested by her brother, Steve, was essential to her accurate and efficient tagging of the cards.

Precautions and Possible Pitfalls

By the age of four or five, most children understand the concept of one-to-one labeling and may be able to count to moderately large numbers. However, this is not necessarily an indication that they appreciate some of the efficiencies provided by appropriate sorting, ordering, or classification. They may also still have difficulty in using such one-to-one labeling with sets of more than five objects. The mastery of such ordering strategies will be essential to their further understanding and exploration of the algebraic structure of our base 10 number system.

Sources

Baroody, A. J., & Wilkins, J. L. M. (1999). The development of informal counting, number, and arithmetic skills and concepts. In Juanita V. Copley (Ed.), *Mathematics in the early years* (pp. 48–65). Reston, VA: NCTM, 1999.

Clements, D. H. (2004). Major themes and recommendations. In D. H. Clements & J. Sarama (Eds.), *Engaging young children in mathematics* (pp. 7–72). Mahwah, NJ: Lawrence Erlbaum.

NCTM. (2000). *Principles and standards for school mathematics*. Reston, VA: NCTM.

STRATEGY 8: Encourage young children's systematic exploration of the general principles and properties of operations such as addition and subtraction.

NCTM Standard

Represent and analyze mathematical situations and structures using algebraic symbols.

What Research and the NCTM Standards Say (NCTM, 2000)

Two central themes of algebraic thinking are appropriate for young students. The first involves making generalizations and using symbols to represent mathematical ideas, and the second is representing and solving problems (Carpenter, Franke, & Levi, 2003). For example, adding pairs of numbers in different orders such as 3 + 5 and 5 + 3 can lead students to infer that when two numbers are added, the order does not matter. As students generalize from observations about numbers and operations, they are forming the basis of algebraic thinking.

Similarly, when students decompose numbers in order to compute, they often use the associative property for the computation. For instance, they may compute 8 + 5, saying, "8 + 2 is 10, and 3 more is 13." Through classroom discussions of different representations during the preK–2 years, children should develop an increased ability to use symbols as a means of recording their thinking. In the earliest years, teachers may provide scaffolding for students by writing for them until they have the ability to record their own ideas.

Classroom Applications

In this vignette (adapted from NCTM, 2000, pp. 93–94), we listen as Ms. Carmichael's kindergartners systematically explore subtractive and additive patterns. Ms. Carmichael has prepared two groups of cards for her kindergarten students. In the first group, the number on the front and back of each card differs by 1. In the second group, these numbers differ by 2.

Ms. Carmichael shows her students a card from the first group with 12 written on it and explains, "On the back of this card, I've written another number." She turns the card over to show the number 13. Then she shows the students a second card with 15 on the front and 16 on the back. As she continues showing the students the cards, each time she asks the students, "What do you think will be on the back?" After a number of cards have been shown, Alison raises her hand and says, "Adding one?" Ms. Carmichael asks the class, "What do you think?" Many of the students agree that Ms. Carmichael was adding 1 to the number on the front to get the number on the back of the card.

Then Ms. Carmichael brings out the second set of cards. These are also numbered front and back, but the numbers differed by 2, for example, 33 and 35, 46 and 48, 22 and 24. Again, she shows the students a sample card and continues with other cards, encouraging them to predict what number is on the back of each card. After she has shown three cards, Jack shouts out, "It's two." Ms. Carmichael reminds him that people weren't to shout out answers and asks the class what they think. A number of students aren't sure. Soon, however, most students figure out that the numbers on the backs of the cards were 2 more than the numbers on the fronts. When the set of cards is exhausted, the students want to play again. "But," Ms. Carmichael says, "we can't do that until I make another set of cards." Alicia speaks up, "You don't have to do that, we can just flip the cards over. The cards will all be minus 2."

In a follow-up to this discussion, Ms. Carmichael might describe what was on each group of cards in a more algebraic manner. For example, the numbers of the backs of the cards in the first group could be named *front number plus 1* and those in the second group *front number plus 2*. Then, building on Alicia's suggestion, the numbers on the backs could be described, respectively, as *front number minus 1* and *front number minus 2*. Such activities have the potential to deepen children's understanding of inverse operational relationships of addition and subtraction.

Precautions and Possible Pitfalls

Although it is not necessary to introduce vocabulary such as *commutativity* or *associativity* in kindergarten, teachers must be aware of the algebraic properties used by students at this age. They should build students' understanding of the importance of their observations about mathematical situations and challenge them to investigate whether specific observations and conjectures hold for all cases. Too often, young children may explore a conjecture for a limited set of numbers (say, numbers less than 20) and fail to recognize that it does not hold for larger numbers.

Sources

Carpenter, T. P., Franke, M. L., & Levi, L. (2003). *Thinking mathematically: Integrating arithmetic and algebra in elementary school*. Portsmouth, NH: Heinemann.
NCTM. (2000). *Principles and standards for school mathematics*. Reston, VA: NCTM.

Grades 3–5

Although *algebra* is a word that has not commonly been heard in Grades 3–5 classrooms, the mathematical investigations and conversations of students in these grades frequently include elements of algebraic reasoning. These experiences and conversations provide rich contexts for advancing mathematical understanding and are also an important precursor to the more formalized study of algebra in the middle and secondary grades. In Grades 3–5, algebraic ideas should emerge and be investigated as students (NCTM, 2000):

- identify or build numerical and geometric patterns
- describe patterns verbally and represent them with tables or symbols
- look for and apply relationships between varying quantities to make predictions
- make and explain generalizations that seem to always work in particular situations
- use graphs to describe patterns and make predictions
- explore number properties
- use invented notation, standard symbols, and variables to express a pattern, generalization, or situation

STRATEGY 9: *Encourage the expression and generalization of mathematics relationships.*

NCTM Standard

Understand patterns, relations, and functions.

What Research and the NCTM Standards Say (NCTM, 2000)

In Grades 3–5, students should investigate numerical and geometric patterns and express them mathematically in words or symbols. They should analyze the structure of the pattern and how it grows or changes, organize this information systematically, and use their analysis to develop generalizations about the mathematical relationships in the pattern (Carpenter, Franke, & Levi, 2003). For example, a teacher might ask students to describe patterns they see in the sequence of square numbers and express the patterns in mathematical sentences:

Figure 2.1

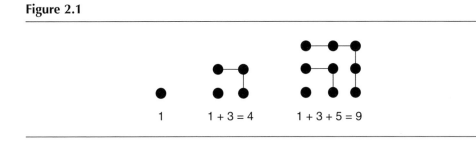

| 1 | 1 + 3 = 4 | 1 + 3 + 5 = 9 |

Examples like this one give the teacher important opportunities to engage students in thinking about how to articulate and express a generalization—for example, "How can we talk about how this pattern works for a square of any size?"

Classroom Applications

In this vignette (adapted from Lampert, 1990), we listen as Ms. Licht's fifth-grade class has a discussion of exponents. Her students have established that all powers of 5 end in 25. They had considered whether powers of 6 end in 36 but had found a counterexample. Luda had proposed that one could figure out the last digits of powers without multiplying the numbers out each time. That is, you don't need to figure out that $5^4 = 625$ in order to know that the last digit is 5.

Ms. Licht asks the class about 7^4. Students agree that the last digit is 1 since "Seven times seven is forty-nine, and nine times nine is eighty-one." Ms. Licht then asks about 7^5. The answers are varied. Mike says that he thinks it is going to be a 1 again; Sarah thinks it will be 9; and Kevin and Heather think it will be 7. Ms. Licht asks Heather, "Why nine, Heather?" Kevin interrupts, "I think they think, maybe, it goes nine, one." Heather says, "I think it is seven because seven to the fourth ends in one and if you multiply it by seven, it'll end in seven." "I think it's seven; no, I think it's eight," says Ronni. Alyias replies, "It can't be eight because an odd number times an odd number is always an odd number." Ms. Licht asks Mike why he thinks it is 1. Mike thinks for a moment and then says, "I want to revise. It's seven times seven times seven times seven times seven. I was thinking that it was seven times seven times seven times one."

Derick raises his hand and says, "I have a proof that it won't be a nine because seven to the third ends in a three." Ronni interrupts, "Oh, I think it goes, 'Seven, nine, one, seven, nine.'" Ms. Licht asks for quiet and turning to Derick asks, "What about seven to the third ending in three? Are you saying that nine times seven is sixty-three?" Derick replies, "It's sort of like what Heather was saying. She said times the last digit by seven and the last digit is nine, so the last one will be three. It's one, seven, nine, three, one, seven, nine, three."

In making generalizations about powers of 7, some of Ms. Licht's students use specific examples as others attempt to express the general sequence. Ms. Licht accepts both strategies while alternately focusing student attention on certain general insights, examples, and counterexamples. In so doing, she provides opportunities for her students to explore ways of expressing and generalizing mathematics relationships.

Precautions and Possible Pitfalls

Encouraging students to explain such patterns and to make predictions and conjectures about what will happen if the pattern is continued can deepen students' mathematics thinking. Fourth graders might be encouraged to make a table and to note the iterative nature of the pattern. Fifth graders might be challenged to justify a proposed general rule (NCTM, 2000). In any case, teachers need to pick numbers and contextual situations that will expand students' experiences of the number structures and associative operations and will challenge students' misconceptions.

Sources

Carpenter, T. P., Franke, M. L., & Levi, L. (2003). *Thinking mathematically: Integrating arithmetic and algebra in elementary school*. Portsmouth, NH: Heinemann.

Lampert, M. (1990). When the problem is not the question and the solution is not the answer. *American Educational Research Journal, 27*, 29–63.

NCTM. (2000). *Principles and standards for school mathematics*. Reston, VA: NCTM.

STRATEGY 10: Encourage further understandings of multiplicative structures through application and analysis of the distributivity of multiplication over addition.

NCTM Standard

Represent and analyze mathematical situations and structures using algebraic symbols.

What Research and the NCTM Standards Say (NCTM, 2000)

In Grades 3–5, students can investigate properties such as commutativity, associativity, and distributivity of multiplication over addition. An area model can help students see that two factors in either order have equal products, as represented by congruent rectangles with different orientations. An area model can also be used to investigate the distributive property. As students learn about the meaning of multiplication and develop strategies to solve multiplication problems, they will begin to use properties such as distributivity naturally (Schifter, 1999). However, discussion about the properties themselves, as well as how they serve as tools for solving a range of problems, is important if students are to add strength to their intuitive notions and advance their understanding of multiplicative structures. Analyzing the properties of operations gives students opportunities to extend their thinking and to build a foundation for applying these understandings to other situations.

Classroom Applications

In this vignette (adapted from Fosnot & Dolk, 2001, pp. 86–88), we listen as Ms. Jensen encourages her fourth-grade students to use computation strategies that draw on the commutative and distributive properties of multiplication.

Ms. Jensen begins by writing $2 \times 3 = ?$ on the chalkboard as her students gather around on the meeting area rug. She smiles as all the students raise their hands and calls on Lara. Lara replies, "Six," and Ms. Jensen, using a small magnet, posts a cutout 2×3 array made from one-inch graph paper next to the problem:

Figure 2.2

Next, Ms. Jensen writes $2 \times 30 = ?$. Again, all her students raise their hands. However, before she calls on anyone, she continues, "Think about what the array will look like. Gabriella?" Gabriella replies, "Sixty." Ms. Jensen repeats, "What will the array look like?" Gabriella replies that it is long and short and that it is thirty plus thirty. Ms. Jensen places a 2×30 array next to the problem.

Figure 2.3

2 ⬜⬜⬜⬜⬜⬜⬜⬜⬜⬜⬜⬜⬜⬜⬜⬜⬜⬜⬜⬜⬜⬜⬜⬜⬜⬜⬜⬜⬜⬜

30

Then Gabriella continues, "You could do it another way, too. It's two times three and then add a zero." Ms. Jensen looks at the class and says "Usually when I add a zero to an amount, I get that amount. Are we really adding a zero? Everybody talk to your neighbors about this. What is happening here?"

Ms. Jensen gives the students a few minutes and then asks Charlie to start the whole-class conversation. Charlie replies, "We think there are really ten two-by-three arrays, but we're not sure." His neighbors and other students nod in agreement. "Well, let's check it out." Ms. Jensen uses the arrays as a model to represent their thinking, iteratively places the 2×3 paper array over the 2×30 array ten times, and marks a line at the end of each iteration.

Figure 2.4

Once the students agree that ten 2×3 arrays fit, she continues with her string of problems, writing 4×4 and then 4×40. She calls on Molly for the latter problem, who replies that it is one hundred and sixty and the array is "four rows of forty, or ten four-by-fours." Ms. Jensen draws a 4×40 rectangle on the board roughly proportional to the 3×30 array.

Next, Ms. Jensen writes "$4 \times 39 = ?$" Olana raises her hand. "I did four times thirty first. That's a hundred and twenty. Then I did four times nine. Together they make a hundred and fifty-six," she explains. Ms. Jensen draws a picture of Olana's thinking:

Figure 2.5

and asks if anybody did it a different way. Gabby says, "I did four times forty first..." Ms. Jensen interrupts and, pointing to the 4×10 rectangle, asks if Gabby started with that array. She says that is what she did, and then at the end she "just took four all away at once."

Figure 2.6

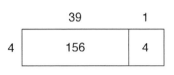

Note that Ms. Jensen carefully structures the discussion so that students are encouraged to apply computational strategies that draw on the associative and distributive properties of multiplication (for further details on this particular technique, see Fosnot & Dolk, 2001):

$2 \times 3 = ?$

$2 \times 30 = ?$ [Students know 2×3]

$4 \times 40 = ?$ [Students know $2 \times 30 = (2 \times 3) \times 10$]

$4 \times 39 = ?$ [Students know 4×40 and 4×30]

In a follow-up to this discussion, Ms. Jensen might have her students explore such questions as: "Why can't twenty-four times thirty-two be solved by adding the results of twenty times thirty and four times two?"

Precautions and Possible Pitfalls

Several algorithms and number strategies in the elementary grades draw on the distributive property of multiplication. The standard algorithm for multiplication:

$$\begin{array}{r} 39 \\ \times\, 4 \\ \hline 156 \end{array}$$

is a straightforward consequence of the distributive property:

$$4 \times 39 = 4 \times (30 + 9)$$
$$= 4 \times 30 + 4 \times 9$$

which, taking into account the 30 that arises in the standard algorithm from 4×9, is

$$= (4 \times 30 + 30) + 6$$

While many fourth-grade students can use the standard algorithm for multiplication to correctly compute 4×39, many are unaware that 4 times the 3 in 39 is 120 rather than 12. An area model, such as that used by Ms. Jensen and her students, can reduce such misconceptions and further deepen students' understandings of place value and multiplication.

Sources

Fosnot, C., & Dolk, M. (2001). *Young mathematicians at work: Constructing multiplication and division.* Portsmouth, NH: Heinemann.

NCTM. (2000). *Principles and standards for school mathematics.* Reston, VA: NCTM.

Schifter, D. (1999). Reasoning about operations: Early algebraic thinking in grades K–6. In L. V. Stiff (Ed.), *Developing mathematical reasoning in Grades K–12, 1999 Yearbook of the National Council of Teachers of Mathematics* (pp. 62–81). Reston, VA: NCTM.

3

Geometry

Grades PreK–2

The geometric and spatial knowledge children bring to school should be expanded by explorations, investigations, and discussions of shapes and structures in the classroom. Students should use their notions of geometric ideas to become more proficient in describing, representing, and navigating their environment. They should learn to represent two- and three-dimensional shapes through drawings, block constructions, dramatizations, and words. They should explore shapes by decomposing them and creating new ones. Their knowledge of direction and position should be refined through the use of spoken language to locate objects by giving and following multistep directions (NCTM, 2000).

Geometry offers students an aspect of mathematical thinking that is different from, but connected to, the world of numbers. As students become familiar with shape, structure, location, and transformations and as they develop spatial reasoning, they lay the foundation for understanding not only their spatial world but also other topics in mathematics and in art, science, and social studies. Some students' capabilities with geometric and spatial concepts exceed their number skills. Building on these strengths fosters enthusiasm for mathematics and provides a context in which to develop number and other mathematics concepts (Razel & Eylon, 1991).

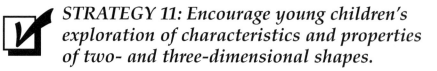

STRATEGY 11: Encourage young children's exploration of characteristics and properties of two- and three-dimensional shapes.

NCTM Standard

Analyze characteristics and properties of two- and three-dimensional geometric shapes and develop mathematical arguments about geometric relationships.

What Research and the NCTM Standards Say (NCTM, 2000)

Children begin forming concepts of shape long before formal schooling. The primary grades are an ideal time to help them refine and extend their understandings. Students first learn to recognize a shape by its appearance as a whole (van Hiele, 1986) or through qualities such as "pointiness" (Lehrer, Jenkins, & Osana, 1998). They may, for example, believe that a given figure is a rectangle because "it looks like a door."

PreK–2 geometry begins with describing and naming shapes. Young students begin by using their own vocabulary to describe objects, talking about how they are alike and how they are different. Teachers must help students gradually incorporate conventional terminology into their descriptions of two- and three-dimensional shapes. However, terminology itself should not be the focus of the preK–2 geometry program. The goal is that early experiences with geometry lay the foundation for more formal geometry in later grades. Using terminology to focus attention and to clarify ideas during discussions can help students build that foundation.

Classroom Applications

During a conversation with a third-grade teacher, Ms. Dolland, a kindergarten teacher, became intrigued by the teacher's account of some lessons she had done using a set of cards with two-dimensional drawings. Some of the shapes on the cards were quite common: a square, a rectangle, and some triangles. Other cards had trapezoids and some familiar shapes—rectangles and triangles—that were not oriented along the horizontal.

Figure 3.1

Because Ms. Dolland wishes to encourage her kindergartners' explorations and knowledge of two-dimensional shapes, she decides to prepare a similar set of cards. In this vignette (adapted from Schifter, Bastable, & Russell, 2002, Case 1), we listen as Ms. Dolland sits with four of her kindergarten students and, as she turns over the cards one at a time, asks them to describe what shape they see and what they know about it.

The first card Ms. Dolland shows has a square. Judy exclaims, "It's a square. It has four sides. They made that language and that's how we speak." Jeanette adds, "It has four sides. It has four corners." Chris says, "It's sort of, you put two skinny rectangles together, it makes one." Cameron speaks up, "Square, because if you put two triangles together, it makes one."

The next card Ms. Dolland shows has a small square oriented in a diamond position. Judy says, "Diamond. It is like having two triangles and two skinny rectangles." Chris adds, "Diamond. If you turn this other one like this (he takes the square that Ms. Dolland had just shown and rotates it so it is tilted), it's the same. I mean, the same, but it's a bigger one because if you put two triangles together, it makes one."

Although young children have had significant experiences with geometric shapes prior to the kindergarten year, they tend to express their geometric understandings with everyday words such as "skinny" or "corner." Activities such as this provide opportunities for students to explore, discuss, and refine their understandings of two-dimensional shapes and, simultaneously, opportunities for teachers to extend such understandings with the timely introduction of appropriate mathematics vocabulary.

Precautions and Possible Pitfalls

It is important for teachers to realize that while a young child may recognize and correctly name shapes drawn on a card or printed in a text, this is only a beginning. For example, young children tend to see rectangles and squares as different shapes, failing to recognize that a square is a rectangle with equal sides. Consequently, young children also need to be given many opportunities to manipulate and sort shapes, as such categorizing of shapes helps them focus on the critical geometric characteristics (Copley, 2000). Young children's ideas about geometric shapes come from exploration: exploration with their bodies, hands, eyes, and minds (Clements, 1999).

Sources

Clements, D. H. (1999). Geometric and spatial thinking in young children. In J. V. Copley (Ed.), *Mathematics in the early years*. Reston, VA: NCTM.

Copley, J. V. (2000). *The young child and mathematics*. Reston, VA: NCTM.

Lehrer, R., Jenkins, M., & Osana, H. (1998).Longitudinal study of children's reasoning about space and geometry. In R. Lehrer & D. Chazan (Eds.), *Designing learning environments for developing understanding of geometry and space* (pp. 137–167). Mahwah, NJ: Erlbaum.

NCTM. (2000). *Principles and standards for school mathematics*. Reston, VA: NCTM.

Razel, M., & Eylon, B. (1991). *Developing mathematics readiness in young children with the Agam Program*. Paper presented at the Fifteenth Conference of the International Group for the Psychology of Mathematics Education, Genoa, Italy.

Schifter, D., Bastable, V., & Russell, S. J. (2002). *Developing mathematical ideas: Examining features of shape*. Parsippany, NJ: Dale Seymour Publications.

van Hiele, P. M. (1986). *Structure and insight: A theory of mathematics education*. Orlando, FL: Academic Press.

STRATEGY 12: *Encourage young children's application of similarity transformations to analyze geometric situations.*

NCTM Standard

Apply transformations and use symmetry to analyze mathematical situations.

What Research and the NCTM Standards Say (NCTM, 2000)

Students can naturally use their own *physical* experiences with shapes to learn about transformations such as slides (translations), turns (rotations), and flips (reflections). They use these movements intuitively when they solve puzzles, turning the pieces, flipping them over, and experimenting with new arrangements (Sophian & Crosby, 1998). Students using interactive computer programs with shapes often have to choose a motion to solve a puzzle. These actions are explorations with transformations and are an important part of spatial learning. They help students become conscious of the motions and encourage them to predict the results of changing a shape's position or orientation but not its size or shape.

Classroom Applications

Ms. Herrera's first grade has done some work during the previous week with pattern blocks. Angela had remarked on how the sharp and flat corners fit together to make other shapes, and Chantilly had noticed triangles within the pattern block shapes.

Figure 3.2

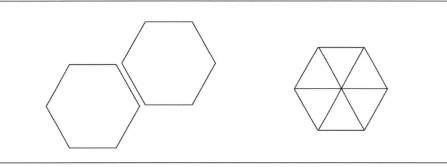

Thus, Ms. Herrera thinks her first graders are ready to explore similarity transformations; she has given the children equilateral triangles, told them to build larger shapes, and asked them to record their answers by tracing the blocks for each shape they make. She has one rule: The sides of the triangles must touch completely. There is a lot of discussion about what it means for sides to touch completely. The consensus is that

Figure 3.3

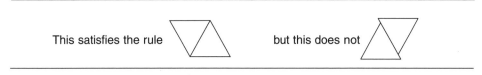

This satisfies the rule   but this does not

Then students go off with their partners to make shapes with the equilateral triangles. In this vignette (adapted from Schifter, Bastable, & Russell, 2002, Case 25), we listen as Ms. Herrera circulates among the students.

Ms. Herrera stops by the table of one threesome—Julius, Olga, and Marjorie—and asks the students what shape they are trying to make. Olga speaks up, "A diamond." Ms. Herrera replies, "Can you show me how you would do that?" Each of the students then makes and traces a diamond with the pattern blocks that uses two triangles, the only difference in their diamonds being orientation.

Figure 3.4

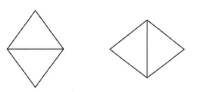

Ms. Herrera asks, "Are these shapes different or the same?" Julius answers, "They're different." Ms. Herrera responds, "Can you explain why?" Marjorie says, "One shape is bigger and one shape is smaller."

Julius adds, "It changes because it gets smaller." Olga interrupts, "They are different because they have different angles." Ms. Herrera asks, "What do you mean by different angles?" Olga replies, "Well, this shape (she points to the horizontal diamond) has its angles facing a different direction than this shape (the vertical diamond). The angle of the shape changes so the shapes are different."

Students often have little experience within the classroom with geometric shapes that are in other-than-standard position, that is, oriented along the vertical or horizontal. Thus, it is not unusual that Ms. Herrera's students see these rhombi as different because the rhombi are pointing in different directions. In her next lesson, Ms. Herrera plans to build on her students' experiences with similarity transformations and have her students use scissors to cut out the drawings. Then she and her class will talk about *same shape* as meaning that one shape can fit exactly over the other.

Precautions and Possible Pitfalls

Although children come to school having informal experiences in flipping, rotating, and sliding shapes, they have not, most usually, been asked to analyze such experiences in any systematic fashion. Thus, they may be puzzled or confused when asked whether two congruent figures oriented differently are the *same* or not—for example, young children often characterize a triangle standing on its vertex as *wrong* (Clements, 1999). Teachers need to provide examples of a variety of geometric shapes in different orientations

Figure 3.5

as well as nonexamples.

Figure 3.6

Computer environments have been found to be particularly effective in developing such analytical skills (Clements, 2003).

Sources

Clements, D. H. (1999). Geometric and spatial thinking in young children. In J. V. Copley (Ed.), *Mathematics in the early years.* Reston, VA: NCTM.

Clements, D. H. (2003). Teaching and learning geometry. In J. Kilpatrick, W. G. Martin, & D. Shifter (Eds.), *A research companion to* Principles and standards for school mathematics. Reston, VA: NCTM.

NCTM. (2000). *Principles and standards for school mathematics.* Reston, VA: NCTM.

Schifter, D., Bastable, V., & Russell, S. J. (2002). *Developing mathematical ideas: Examining features of shape.* Parsippany, NJ: Dale Seymour Publications.

Sophian, C., & Crosby, M. E. (1998, August). *Ratios that even young children understand: The case of spatial proportions.* Paper presented at the meeting of the Cognitive Society of Dublin, Ireland.

STRATEGY 13: *Encourage young children's use of visualization and spatial reasoning in their exploration of geometric shapes.*

NCTM Standard

Use visualization, spatial reasoning, and geometric modeling to solve problems.

What Research and the NCTM Standards Say (NCTM, 2000)

Spatial visualization can be developed by building and manipulating first concrete and then mental representations of shapes, relationships, and transformations (Clements & Battista, 1992). Teachers should plan instruction so that students can explore the relationships of different attributes or change one characteristic of a shape while preserving others. Conversations about what they notice and how to change from one shape to another allow students to hear different points of view and at the same time give teachers insight into their students' understanding. Work with concrete shapes lays a valuable foundation for spatial sense. To further develop students' abilities, teachers might ask them to see in their "mind's eye" the shapes that would result when a shape is flipped or when a square is cut diagonally from corner to corner. Thus, many shape and transformation activities build spatial reasoning if students are asked to imagine, predict, experiment, and check the results of the work themselves.

Classroom Applications

 For the past three weeks, Ms. Román's kindergartners have been using a set of wooden geometric solids for geometry work.

Figure 3.7

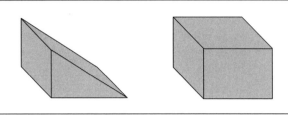

Some students have built towers, some have combined blocks to create other shapes—for instance, joining two triangular prisms to create a rectangular prism. In this vignette (adapted from Schifter, Bastable, & Russell, 2002, Case 5), we listen in as Ms. Román encourages her students to use visualization and spatial reasoning to focus on the attributes of the solids.

Ms. Román holds up a rectangular prism and turns it slowly for all to see.

Figure 3.8

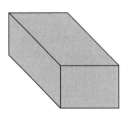

She asks, "What do you notice about this block?" Pat speaks up, "It is a rectangle." Derrick adds, "It has six sides." Lourdes says, "It has two long sides and two short sides." Pat says, "It looks like a box." Ms. Román says, "I would like everyone to come up to the blocks bin and find a block that also looks like a box."

About half the class easily picks out a boxlike block. Each of them looks carefully as they make a choice, offering comments as they pick up and examine each block. Cynthia says, "Mine is a skinny box." Erica replies, "Mine is larger than yours." Jack notes, "Mine is a square box." Pat adds, "Mine is, too. Two of mine equals yours (she points to the block Ms. Román holds). Ms. Román asks, "Why do you think that, Pat?" Pat says, "'Cause mine is half of yours, so I need two!"

Figure 3.9

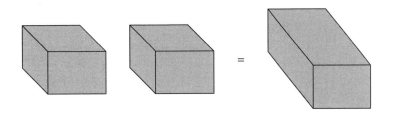

As in most primary classrooms, Ms. Román's students are simultaneously working on several different conceptual levels; that is, the class focuses, in turn, on the dimensions of the blocks, the shape of the blocks, and the volume of the blocks. Activities such as this and the corresponding student comments can be productively probed—for example, Ms. Román might ask Pat to show the class what she means by "half of yours"—in ways that substantially enhance spatial reasoning for the entire class.

Precautions and Possible Pitfalls

 Children in their simple naming of geometric objects often focus unreflectively on simple surface level categories—for example, *skinny* or *larger*. Teachers need to provide opportunities for children to manipulate dynamic images so that they move beyond such simple visual thinking and become able to systematically connect their knowledge of shapes to verbal mathematical knowledge. Manipulative work with shapes—for example, pattern blocks or tangrams—has been found to be effective in developing such connections (Clements, 1999). Teachers can also ask children to identify objects or structures from various viewpoints and match views of the same object portrayed from different perspectives.

Sources

Clements, D. H. (1999). Geometric and spatial thinking in young children. In J. V. Copley (Ed.), *Mathematics in the early years*. Reston, VA: NCTM.

Clements, D. H., & Battista, M. T. (1992). Geometry and spatial reasoning. In D. A. Grouws (Ed.), *Handbook of research on mathematics teaching and learning* (pp. 420–464). New York: Macmillian.

NCTM. (2000). *Principles and standards for school mathematics*. Reston, VA: NCTM.

Schifter, D., Bastable, V., & Russell, S. J. (2002). *Developing mathematical ideas: Examining features of shape*. Parsippany, NJ: Dale Seymour Publications.

Grades 3–5

The reasoning skills that students develop in Grades 3–5 allow them to investigate geometric problems of increasing complexity and to study geometric properties. As they move from Grade 3 to Grade 5, they should develop clarity and precision in describing the properties of geometric objects and then classifying them by these properties into categories such as rectangle, triangle, pyramid, or prism. They can develop knowledge about how geometric shapes are related to one another and begin to articulate geometric arguments about the properties of these shapes. They should also explore motion, location, and orientation by, for example, creating paths on a coordinate grid or defining a series of flips and turns to demonstrate that two shapes are congruent. As students investigate geometric properties and relationships, their work can be closely connected with other mathematical topics, especially measurement and numbers.

The study of geometry in Grades 3–5 requires thinking and doing. As students sort, build, draw, model, trace, measure, and construct, their capacity to visualize geometric relationships will develop. At the same time, they are learning to reason and to make, test, and justify conjectures about these relationships. This exploration requires access to a variety of tools, such as graph paper, rulers, pattern blocks, geoboards, and geometric solids, and is greatly enhanced by electronic tools that support exploration, such as dynamic geometry software (NCTM, 2000).

STRATEGY 14: Encourage students' exploration and mathematical analysis of the properties of two-dimensional geometric shapes.

NCTM Standard

Analyze characteristics and properties of two- and three-dimensional geometric shapes and develop mathematical arguments about geometric relationships.

What Research and the NCTM Standards Say (NCTM, 2000)

In the early grades, students will have classified and sorted geometric objects such as triangles or cylinders by noting general characteristics. In Grades 3–5, they should develop more precise ways to describe shapes, focusing on identifying and describing the shapes' properties and learning specialized vocabulary associated with these shapes and properties. To consolidate their ideas, students should draw and construct shapes, compare and discuss their attributes, classify them, and develop and consider definitions on the basis of a shape's properties, such as that a rectangle has four straight sides and four square corners (Clements, 2003).

In Grades 3–5, teachers should emphasize the development of mathematical arguments. As students' ideas about shapes evolve, they should formulate conjectures about geometric properties and relationships. Using drawings, concrete materials, and geometry software to develop and test their ideas, they can articulate clear mathematical arguments about why geometric relationships are true. For example: "You can't possibly make a triangle with two right angles because if you start with one side of the triangle across the bottom, the other two sides go straight up. They're parallel, so they can't possibly ever meet, so you can't get it to be a triangle."

Classroom Applications

Ms. Diaz is beginning a geometry unit with her fifth graders. Because she wishes to deepen and challenge her students' notions of shapes and their properties, she decides to initially guide them in an exploration of the mathematical definition of quadrilateral. In this vignette (adapted from NCTM, 1991, Vignette 2.2), we listen as Ms. Diaz begins the lesson.

Ms. Diaz announces, "We're going to be studying quadrilaterals. What do you know about quadrilaterals?" Several students chorus, "Four sides, four-sided figure." Ms. Diaz draws

Figure 3.10

and asks, "Is this one?" Her students reply, "No, it has to connect." Ms. Diaz draws and asks, "Is this one?"

Figure 3.11

Several students say, "No, it can't intersect like that." Ms. Diaz continues drawing and asks, "So is this one?"

Figure 3.12

Alison replies, "It has to close." Ms. Diaz asks, "Okay, then is this one?"

Figure 3.13

A number of students seem unsure. Ms. Diaz asks, "Is this one?"

Figure 3.14

All the students say, "Yes."

Ms. Diaz pauses and then looks directly at her class. "I drew five examples. You said three of these didn't work. Can you explain what makes the difference?" As students volunteer pieces of a definition of quadrilateral, Ms. Diaz lists their ideas—in their terms—on the board:

QUADRILATERALS

4 points

4 segments

no more points intersect

closed curve

Summarizing, Ms. Diaz tells her class, "Nice thinking, the definition in our text is *the union of segments joining four points such that the segments intersect only at the endpoints.*"

Ms. Diaz's students came to the fifth grade with considerable expertise in the sorting and classification of geometric objects. However, they may not have had the opportunity to carefully reflect on the significance of the geometric definitions they have learned. Activities such as this encourage mathematical analysis of two-dimensional shapes and provide experience in mathematical thinking.

Precautions and Possible Pitfalls

 Although such an activity can be helpful in clarifying students' understanding of a particular definition, it is only a beginning. Students need opportunities to propose their own mathematical classifications. As a case in point, after clarifying the definition of quadrilateral, Ms. Diaz draws several figures on the board—a trapezoid, a rectangle, and a square—and asks her students to work in pairs and classify these figures. Marc raises his hand. "But isn't a square also a rectangle? I don't quite see how to classify these." Ms. Diaz replies to the class, "What do you think about Marc's question? See if you can find a way to classify these shapes. What shapes have which labels?"

Note that Ms. Diaz purposively does not respond to Marc's question nor does she further clarify her directions. The purpose of this activity is to encourage children to do their own mathematical exploration of these two dimensional shapes and to propose their own classifications. Children, with appropriate experiences and guidance, can learn to classify figures hierarchically by ordering their properties and can learn to give informal arguments to justify such classifications (Clements, 2003).

Sources

Clements, D. H. (2003). Teaching and learning geometry. In J. Kilpatrick, W. G. Martin, & D. Shifter (Eds.), *A research companion to* Principles and standards for school mathematics. Reston, VA: NCTM.

NCTM. (1991). *Professional standards for teaching mathematics.* Reston, VA: NCTM.

NCTM (2000). *Principles and standards for school mathematics.* Reston, VA: NCTM.

 STRATEGY 15: Encourage students' use of geometric transformations to analyze mathematical situations.

NCTM Standard

Apply transformations and use symmetry to analyze mathematical situations.

What Research and the NCTM Standards Say (NCTM, 2000)

Students in Grades 3–5 should consider three important kinds of transformations: reflections, translations, and rotations (flips, slides, and turns). Younger students generally "prove" (that is, convince themselves) that two shapes are congruent by physically fitting one on top of the other, but students in Grades 3–5 can develop greater precision as they describe the motions needed to show congruence ("turn it 90 degrees" or "flip it vertically, then rotate it 180 degrees"). They should also be able to visualize what will happen when a shape is rotated or reflected and predict the result (Clements, 2003).

Classroom Applications

Ms. Faulk has designed a series of activities to help her third graders better understand rotational and mirror symmetry. In this beginning activity, Ms. Faulk has given each of her students toothpicks and asked them to find all the different ways of arranging them in groups of four so that each toothpick touches the end of at least one other toothpick, and each toothpick is placed either end to end or so that it makes square corners. In this vignette (adapted from Burns & Tank, 1988, Explorations With Four Toothpicks*), we listen as Ms. Faulk asks if somebody can arrange the toothpicks in a way that fits the rules.*

Cassandra raises her hand. "You can make a square." Ms. Faulk does so with four toothpicks, dipping the ends of the toothpicks into a small cup of glue and placing them on construction paper that has been cut into 6" × 9" rectangles. Rick raises his hand. "You can make an F," he suggests. Ms. Faulk glues four toothpicks to a piece of construction paper in the shape of an F.

Figure 3.15

Ms. Faulk asks if somebody can make a different shape. Marc points to the F and says, "Just turn it upside down." Ms. Faulk takes the piece of construction paper and turns it upside down and says, "This is the same as Rick suggested. Who can explain why?" Several students offer explanations: "It's turned around." "It's still an F."

Ms. Faulk then takes four toothpicks and creates a mirror image of the F.

Figure 3.16

She says, "This one is also the same as the F. Why do you think that's so?" Some of the children notice that it is a backwards F, but others are perplexed. Ms. Faulk turns the paper with the F over and holds it up to the window.

Figure 3.17

This  becomes this

She says, "If you flip a shape and then it matches another, they're considered the same. You can check to see if your shape is different by drawing it, turning it over, and holding it up to the window."

Ms. Faulk has designed a series of activities that build on students' informal notions of transformation and symmetry. This first activity provides a context in which students can begin to explore more formal notions of rotation and symmetry. Ms. Faulk might, in subsequent lessons, ask her students to demonstrate—by applying transformations—how, for example, the following are the *same:*

Figure 3.18

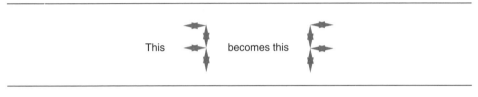

Precautions and Possible Pitfalls

 Teachers should note that while many children appear to be quite capable of performing the manual procedures for producing transformational images, this does not indicate that they are able to do so mentally. Nonetheless, there are indications that students can, given appropriate experiences and guidance, internalize these motions and use them for analyzing mathematical situations. Computer environments—such as Turtle Math or Geometer's Sketchpad—can be effective in the development of such skills when children are given opportunities to discuss and reflect on the construction of symmetric figures and on the properties of symmetries (Clements, 2003).

Sources

Burns, M., & Tank, B. (1988). *A collection of math lessons: From Grades 1 through 3.* Sausalito, CA: Math Solution Publications.

Clements, D. H. (2003). Teaching and learning geometry. In J. Kilpatrick, W. G. Martin, & D. Shifter (Eds.), *A research companion to* Principles and standards for school mathematics. Reston, VA: NCTM.

NCTM. (2000). *Principles and standards for school mathematics.* Reston, VA: NCTM.

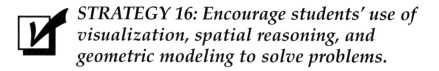

STRATEGY 16: Encourage students' use of visualization, spatial reasoning, and geometric modeling to solve problems.

NCTM Standard

Use visualization, spatial reasoning, and geometric modeling to solve problems.

What Research and the NCTM Standards Say (NCTM, 2000)

Students in Grades 3–5 should examine the properties of two- and three-dimensional shapes and the relationships among shapes. They should be encouraged to reason about these properties by using spatial relationships. For instance, they might reason about the area of a triangle by visualizing its relationship to a corresponding rectangle or other corresponding parallelogram.

Figure 3.19

In addition to studying physical models of these geometric shapes, they should also develop and use mental images. Students at this age are ready to mentally manipulate shapes, and they can benefit from experiences that challenge them and that can also be verified physically (Clements & Battista, 1992). For example, "Draw a star in the upper right-hand corner of a piece of paper. If you flip the paper horizontally and then turn it 180 degrees, where will the star be?"

Figure 3.20

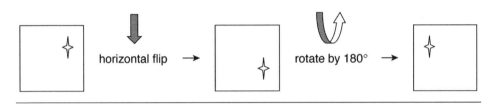

Much of the work students do with three-dimensional shapes involves visualization. By representing three-dimensional shapes in two dimensions and constructing three-dimensional shapes from two-dimensional representations, students learn about the characteristics of shapes. For example, in order to determine if this two-dimensional shape

Figure 3.21

is a net that can be folded into a cube, students need to pay attention to the number, shape, and relative positions of its faces.

Classroom Applications

Ms. Schopp wishes to encourage her students' use of visualization and spatial reasoning. She decides that a useful activity might be helping her fourth graders make sense of three-dimensional shapes and the two-dimensional drawings that are used to represent them. In this lesson, one of the problems Ms. Schopp has posed for her students is which of the following patterns can be folded up to make an open box:

Figure 3.22

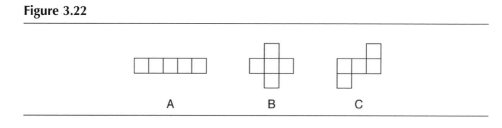

A   B   C

That is, the three-dimensional figure

Figure 3.23

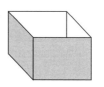

As Ms. Schopp walks around the classroom, she notices that many of her students just glance at the patterns and write yes or no. In this vignette (adapted from Schifter, Bastable, & Russell, 2002, Case 31), we listen in as the class discusses the problem.

Ms. Schopp asks Norman how he figured out his answer. Norman replies, "I folded the shapes in my mind." A number of the other students nod their agreement. In general, her students seem to agree which shapes can be folded to make a box. However, they have difficulty in explaining the process. Suddenly, Agnes speaks up, "Shape A is an array and B and C aren't."

Ms. Schopp takes three of the array cards the students had used in their multiplication unit and displays them in front of the class.

Figure 3.24

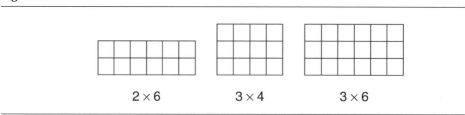

2 × 6   3 × 4   3 × 6

She says, "Is there an array that is also a box pattern? Let's look at some of the arrays we used in our work on multiplication to see what we notice." The students look at the arrays carefully. Then Sonia waves her hand excitedly. "I think I figured out how to make one! . . . Never mind."

Trevor picks up the 3×6 array and starts to fold it saying, "Well, you could chop off the sides." Agnes exclaims, "Then it won't be an array." Trevor says, "Well, then can you cut some of it? Maybe not a whole square?" Ms. Schopp tells him to try, but even then, he can't seem to make a box.

Norman raises his hand. "I think I might know. Well, not the answer, but I think it's no. Because if you fold the sides up, you can't fold the end." He hesitates and then continues, "And if you fold the ends up, you can't fold the sides up." Agnes adds, "When I think of an array, the corners always get in the way."

Ms. Schopp has provided an experience that encourages her students to use visualization and spatial reasoning to mentally construct a three-dimensional object from its unfolded two-dimensional representation. In a following lesson, she will have her students take apart boxes for recycling and sketch the two-dimensional shapes that are formed.

Precautions and Possible Pitfalls

Although students may display an intuition that some geometric conjecture is, in fact, true, there is yet a large step from that intuition to constructing an appropriately convincing mathematical argument. For example, to determine whether one of Ms. Schopp's patterns can be folded into a box, her students need to systematically consider the number, shape, and relative positions of its faces. The language used by some of Ms. Schopp's students—for example, "When I think of an array, the corners always get in the way"—indicates that several are attempting to take that step. However, her students will need multiple opportunities to test and express their ideas.

Sources

Clements, D. H., & Battista, M. T. (1992). Geometry and spatial reasoning. In D. A. Grouws (Ed.), *Handbook of research on mathematics teaching and learning* (pp. 420–464). New York: Macmillian.

NCTM. (2000). *Principles and standards for school mathematics*. Reston, VA: NCTM.

Schifter, D., Bastable, V., & Russell, S. J. (2002). *Developing mathematical ideas: Examining features of shape*. Parsippany, NJ: Dale Seymour Publications.

4

Measurement

Grades PreK–2

Measurement is one of the most widely used applications of mathematics. It bridges two main areas of school mathematics—geometry and numbers. Measurement activities can simultaneously teach important everyday skills, strengthen students' knowledge of other important topics in mathematics, and develop measurement concepts and processes that will be formalized and expanded in later years.

Teaching that builds on students' intuitive understandings and informal measurement experiences helps them understand the attributes to be measured as well as what it means to measure. A foundation in measurement concepts that enables students to use measurement systems, tools, and techniques should be established through direct experiences with comparing objects, counting units, and making connections between spatial concepts and numbers (NCTM, 2000).

STRATEGY 17: *Encourage young children's exploration and understanding of measurement concepts and relationships.*

NCTM Standard

 Understand measurable attributes of objects and the units, systems, and processes of measurement.

What Research and the NCTM Standards Say (NCTM, 2000)

Children often begin to develop an understanding of attributes by looking at, touching, or directly comparing objects (Lindquist, 1989; Piaget, Inhelder, & Szeminska, 1960). They can determine who has more by looking at the size of piles of objects or identify which of two objects is heavier by picking them up. They can compare shoes, placing them side-by-side, to check which is longer. Adults should help young children recognize attributes through their conversations. "That is a deep hole." "Let's put the toys in the large box." "That is a long piece of rope." In school, students continue to learn about attributes as they describe objects, compare them, and order them by different attributes. Seeing order relationships, such as that the soccer ball is bigger than the baseball but smaller than the beach ball, is important in developing measurement concepts.

Classroom Applications

Teachers can guide young children's exploration and understanding of measurement concepts and relationships by making resources for measuring available, planning opportunities to measure, and encouraging children to explain the results of their actions.

In this vignette (adapted from Schifter, Bastable, & Russell, 2002, Case 5), we listen as Ms. Askew encourages her kindergartners to explore the idea of volume. Ms. Askew has constructed two topless cardboard boxes for her students to measure. Box A (40 cubic inches in volume) is ten inches long, four inches wide, and one inch deep. Box B (72 cubic inches in volume) is six inches long, four inches wise, and three inches deep. Ms. Askew plans to have her students use one-inch cubes to fill the boxes.

Her students seem quite curious as she sets them on the table and asks, "Which box do you think is bigger? How do you know which one is bigger?" Lori points to box A and says, "That one is longer." She then points to box B and says, "That one is taller." Jack notes, "They are bigger in different ways." Ms. Askew asks, "Which one holds more?" The students seem unsure. Some point to box A, some to box B, and some think the boxes hold the same amount. Jason moves the boxes so that the four-inch sides are aligned and remarks, "These are the same." However, Norman, moving the boxes so that the longest sides are aligned, objects, "But it's not the same length." Ms. Askew says, "How could we find out which box holds more?" Norman, pointing to the basket of one-inch cubes on the table, replies, "By just putting them in."

The students, working in small groups, begin filling the boxes. At first, some students put cubes randomly into the boxes. However, after some discussion with their neighbors, all students begin carefully stacking cubes so that there are no gaps. Aida, pointing at box B, remarks to Craig, "I think that one is going to hold more." Craig replies, "I think they'll hold the same amount." Aida thinks for a moment and then says, "Maybe we can count." Soon all the students have filled the boxes and some have begun counting. Lori, counting the cubes in box B by threes, reaches 72. "Wow!" says Craig, pointing at box A, "That one has only forty." He points at box B and says, "This one has more."

Ms. Askew has provided a mathematics context in which children are encouraged to test their preconceptions as to what effectively constitutes volume and encouraged to develop strategies for its measurement. Experiences such as this are useful in building both procedural and conceptual knowledge of measurement.

Precautions and Possible Pitfalls

Measurement has its roots in everyday life. However, in addition to being something a person does, it requires imagination. That is, a young child must be able to imagine or assume qualities of the world such as space and time. Thus, although a young child may demonstrate considerable facility with counting, this does not mean that he or she understands space or time measure (Lehrer, 2003). Such understandings are the product of many experiences and explorations of space and time.

Sources

Lehrer, R. (2003). Developing understanding of measurement. In J. Kilpatrick, W. G. Martin, & D. Shifter (Eds.), *A research companion to* Principles and standards for school mathematics. Reston, VA: NCTM.

Lindquist, M. (1989). The measurements standards. *Arithmetic Teacher, 37*(1), 22–26.

NCTM. (2000). *Principles and standards for school mathematics*. Reston, VA: NCTM.

Piaget, J., Inhelder, B., & Szeminska, A. (1960). *The child's conception of geometry*. New York: Basic Books.

Schifter, D., Bastable, V., & Russell, S. J. (2002). *Developing mathematical ideas: Measuring space in one, two, and three dimensions*. Parsippany, NJ: Dale Seymour Publications.

STRATEGY 18: Encourage young children to accurately apply appropriate tools and techniques to linear measurement.

NCTM Standard

Apply appropriate techniques, tools, and formulas to determine measurements.

What Research and the NCTM Standards Say (NCTM, 2000)

Measurement concepts and skills can develop together as students position multiple copies of the same units without leaving spaces between them or as they measure by iterating one unit without overlapping or leaving gaps. Both types of experiences are necessary (Horvath & Lehrer, 2000; Lehrer, Jenkins, & Osana, 1998). Similarly, using rulers, students learn concepts and procedures, including accurate alignment (e.g., ignoring the leading edge at the beginning of many rulers), starting at zero, and focusing on the lengths of the units rather than only on the numbers on the ruler. By emphasizing the question "What are you counting?", teachers help students focus on the meaning of the measurements they are making.

Classroom Applications

Teachers, by providing many varied experiences, can encourage the development of skills and dispositions such as accurate use of tools and self-questioning when measurements may not be sufficiently accurate. In this vignette (adapted from NCTM, 2000, p. 106), we listen as Ms. Lambrech's second graders are encouraged to explore appropriate tools and techniques for linear measurement. Ms. Lambrech has given her students a list of things to measure and has left the choice of measuring tools up to them.

Matsa is using a ruler when Ms. Lambrech stops by her desk to observe her measuring her book. "It's twelve inches," Matsa says as she writes the measurement on the recording sheet. Next she measures her pencil, which was noticeably shorter than the book. Ms. Lambrech notices that Matsa's hand slips as she is aligning her ruler with the pencil, but Matsa makes no comment and records this measurement as twelve inches also.

Ms. Lambrech says, "I notice that you wrote that each of these is twelve inches. I'm confused. The book looks much longer than the pencil to me. What do you think?" Matsa pushes both items close together and studies them. "You're right," she says. "The book is longer, but they are both twelve inches." Pearl, who is sitting nearby, interrupts, "You have to start from the beginning." "What do you mean, Pearl?" asks Ms. Lambrech. Pearl points to the first mark on the ruler. Matsa, who is listening, aligns the pencil with the first mark on the ruler and records the measurement as five inches.

Ms. Lambrech, by emphasizing the object Matsa is measuring, refocuses Matsa's awareness on the meaning of the measurements. This moment with Matsa also alerts Ms. Lambrech to an accuracy issue that might be productively addressed in future discussions with Matsa and the class. She might, for example, ask her students to pair up when doing their measurements.

Precautions and Possible Pitfalls

Teachers cannot assume that students understand measurement fully even when they are able to tell how long an object is when it is aligned with a ruler. Second graders may, for example, freely mix inches and centimeters, counting all to measure a length (Lehrer, Jenkins, & Osana, 1998). Using tools accurately, questioning when measurements may not be accurate, and understanding unit-attribute relationships require concepts and skills that develop over extended periods through many varied experiences.

Sources

Horvath, J., & Lehrer, R. (2000). The design of a case-based hypermedia teaching tool. *International Journal of Computers for Mathematical Learning, 5,* 115–141.

Lehrer, R., Jenkins, M., & Osana, H. (1998). Longitudinal study of children's reasoning about space and geometry. In R. Lehrer & D. Chazan (Eds.), *Designing learning environments for developing understanding of geometry and space* (pp. 169–200). Mahwah, NJ: Erlbaum.

NCTM. (2000). *Principles and standards for school mathematics.* Reston, VA: NCTM.

Grades 3–5

Measurement is a process that students in Grades 3–5 use every day as they explore questions related to their school or home environment. For example, how much catsup is used in the school cafeteria each day? What is the distance from my house to the school? What is the range of heights of players on the basketball team? Such questions require students to use concepts and tools of measurement to collect data and to describe and quantify their world. In Grades 3–5, measurement helps connect ideas within areas of mathematics and between mathematics and other disciplines. It can serve as a context to help students understand important mathematical concepts such as fractions, geometric shapes, and ways of describing data.

Prior to Grade 3, students should have begun to develop an understanding of what it means to measure an object; that is, identifying an attribute to be measured, choosing an appropriate unit, and comparing that unit to the object being measured. They should have had many experiences with measuring length and should also have explored ways to measure liquid volume, weight, and time. In Grades 3–5, students should deepen and expand their understanding and use of measurement. For example, they should measure other attributes such as area and angle. They need to begin paying closer attention to the degree of accuracy when measuring and use a wider variety of measurement tools. They should also begin to develop and use formulas for the measurement of certain attributes, such as area (NCTM, 2000).

STRATEGY 19: *Encourage students' exploration and understanding of measurement concepts and relationships.*

NCTM Standard

Understand measurable attributes of objects and the units, systems, and processes of measurement.

What Research and the NCTM Standards Say (NCTM, 2000)

Students in Grades 3–5 should measure the attributes of a variety of physical objects and extend their work to measuring more complex attributes, including area, volume, and angle. Such mathematics work affords opportunities for developing ideas about the curvature and dimensionality of space (Lehrer, 2003). Students will also learn that length measurements in particular contexts are given specific names, such as perimeter, width, height, circumference, and distance. They can begin to establish some benchmarks by which to estimate or judge the size of objects. For example, they learn that a "square corner" is called a right angle and establish this as a benchmark for estimating the size of other angles.

Students in Grades 3–5 should explore how measurements are affected when one attribute to be measured is held constant and the other is changed. For example, suppose you had sixty-four meters of fence with which you were going to build a pen for your large dog, Rusty. What are some of the pens you can make if you use all the fencing? What is the pen with the least play space? What is the pen with the largest? Such activities as this provide opportunities to discuss the relationship of area to perimeter (NCTM, 1991).

Classroom Applications

During the week before spring vacation, Ms. Brito began a project designed to encourage her third graders' exploration and understanding of area and perimeter. In order to contextualize the activity, she has given her third-grade students construction cutouts of irregular shapes representing ponds and told them a story about Carlos and Vanessa who want to choose the largest pond for their skating rink. Over the next few days, her students worked with partners exploring, with various uniform and plane-filling manipulatives (such as square tiles), ways to measure the area of the ponds. Many of her students come to see that measuring the linear distance across the ponds or the perimeter does not necessarily allow them to compare the area of the ponds. In this vignette (adapted from Schifter, Bastable, & Russell, 2002, Case 30), we listen as Ms. Brito is asking her students to measure the areas of a set of rectangles—three inches by twelve inches, two inches by eighteen inches, and six inches by six inches.

Ms. Brito begins by listing the various ways students have used to measure the ponds—that is, measuring the length and width with a ruler, measuring the perimeter, and covering the inner space with uniform manipulatives—and then shows her students the nine-inch by four-inch rectangle. She notes that it has been hard to figure out the areas of the irregular shapes and that working with rectangles will be easier and says, "Some kids think that if you measure the perimeter of the pond, you can judge the space inside. But we haven't found the rulers to be too helpful in comparing the ponds' space for skating. What could we use to measure the space covered by this rectangular pond? Keep in mind that a ruler measures lines."

Corey speaks up, "The tiles because they're inch by inch." Ms. Brito replies, "Mathematicians use square inches, just like these tiles, to measure area." She then asks the class which of the ways she has listed will, most likely, help compare the areas of the two rectangular ponds. Kelly responds, "Perimeter won't help us. You can have a really big perimeter with lots of jogs and not much area inside." "Yeah," adds Roseline, "perimeter and area are not related. You can have a long perimeter and not much skating space."

Ms. Brito has the students choose one of the rectangles with a partner, pick up rulers and square-inch tiles, and set to work. Later, as the class gathers together in a group and looks at their measurements, her students seem satisfied as well as surprised by some of the findings. Derrick, for example, is quite surprised by the fact that the rectangles had different perimeters and the same area. "Ours has a perimeter of thirty and an area of thirty-six, but this other one has a perimeter of forty and still an area of thirty-six. And look at this one. It has a perimeter of twenty-four and an area of thirty-six. How can that be?" "That's ours," says Kelly. "It's right. See, it's a square. The perimeter is all sixes, so that's six plus six equals twelve and twelve plus twelve equals twenty-four, so it's right. And the area is thirty-six. We counted the tiles. It's right."

Ms. Brito has provided an opportunity for her students to look more deeply into the procedures and concepts that underlie area measurement. Her choice to begin the project by having her students attempt to compare the area of irregular figures provides the need for a uniform plane-filling unit and encourages her students to use such a unit in devising measurement strategies. Once these foundations are in place, she encourages her students to explore the relationships between area and linear measure in regular geometric shapes.

Precautions and Possible Pitfalls

Frequently, rectangular area is treated in school as a simple matter of multiplying length and width, but research suggests that many children do not understand this product to be a measurement nor do they understand that a rectangle might be structured as an array of unit squares. Often, children focus on the boundaries of objects rather than the space the object occupies and treat length as a space-filling attribute (Lehrer, 2003). Children need experiences that both challenge these habits and require them to measure with space-filling objects such as tiles.

Sources

Lehrer, R. (2003). Developing understanding of measurement. In J. Kilpatrick, W. G. Martin, & D. Shifter (Eds.), *A research companion to* Principles and standards for school mathematics. Reston, VA: NCTM.
NCTM. (1991). *Professional standards for teaching mathematics.* Reston, VA: NCTM.
NCTM. (2000). *Principles and standards for school mathematics.* Reston, VA: NCTM.
Schifter, D., Bastable, V., & Russell, S. J. (2002). *Developing mathematical ideas: Measuring space in one, two, and three dimensions.* Parsippany, NJ: Dale Seymour Publications.

 STRATEGY 20: Encourage students' appropriate application of conventional measuring tools in varied situations.

NCTM Standard

 Apply appropriate techniques, tools, and formulas to determine measurements.

What Research and the NCTM Standards Say (NCTM, 2000)

In Grades 3–5, an expanded number of tools and range of measurement techniques should be available to students. When using conventional tools such as rulers and tape measures for measuring length, students will need instruction to learn to use these tools properly (Lehrer et al., 1998). For example, they will need to recognize and understand the markings on a ruler, including where the "0," or beginning point, is located. When standard measurement tools are difficult to use in a particular situation, they must learn to adapt their tools or invent techniques that will work.

Students in Grades 3–5 should develop strategies to estimate measurements. For example, to estimate the length of the classroom, they might estimate the length of one floor tile and then count the number of tiles across the room and multiply the length by the number of tiles. Another strategy for estimating measurements is to compare the item to be measured against some benchmark. For example, a student might estimate the teacher's height by noting that it is about one and a quarter times the student's own height. This particular strategy highlights the use of multiplicative reasoning, an important indication of advancing understanding.

Classroom Applications

Ms. Slagle wishes to encourage her fourth graders' appropriate use of a ruler in varied situations calling for linear measurement and has designed an activity that requires her students to measure one object in class each week and record their measurements on a chart on the math bulletin board. The only limitations are that students choose something that could be measured by a ruler, yardstick, meter stick, or tape measure, and that could be measured without climbing or otherwise risking harm. In this vignette (adapted from Schifter, Bastable, & Russell, 2002, Case 16), we listen as Ms. Slagle, choosing as examples the measurements done by Julius, Eva, and Craig, discusses with her class how one might do the measurements, what tools they might use, and the relative accuracy of their measurements.

Eva had measured the length of the chalkboard with a meter stick by successively using the thirty-nine-inch line on the inch side of the meter stick. When she demonstrates her measurement strategy for the class, she forgets this and makes her successive marks at the ends of the meter stick. Thus, her new total is different from her original total. Noticing this, Yamile points out that Eva's marks are not accurate "because of the little extra at the end of the meter stick." When Yamile and Eva apply this correction and remeasure the chalkboard, their new measurement agrees with Eva's original measurement.

Eva's mistake and correction leads to a class discussion on the way to use a ruler, yardstick, or meter stick. In the midst of the discussion, Craig explains, "You need to start at the zero. The end of the ruler, before the one, is zero." Ms. Slagle points out that there is no zero on the ruler and asks for somebody to explain what Craig means. Derick replies, "They didn't put it there, but at the beginning of the ruler there is a zero." Ms. Slagle says that she still doesn't see a zero. Ana responds, "Because when you start at one on a tape measure or something, you already have one inch." "Yeah," says Craig, "the number one is at the end of one inch, not at the beginning."

By having her students develop and share their measuring strategies, Ms. Slagle encourages the comparison and evaluation of different approaches. Simultaneously, the development of iterative measurement strategies—for example, the strategy used by Eva—can usefully further multiplicative reasoning.

Precautions and Possible Pitfalls

There is a deep connection between modeling space and exploring its extent. A child must construct a model—for instance, the linear model of the chalkboard—and then use tools—for instance, the meter stick—to measure its attributes. However, such tools can be used inappropriately. Children may simply read off whatever number on a ruler aligns with the end of an object (Lehrer et al., 1998). If children are to use such tools appropriately, they need experiences in which they are required to take account of the inherent imprecision of measurement.

Sources

Lehrer, R., Jacobsen, C., Thoyre, G., Kemeny, V., Strom, D., Horvath, J., Gance, S., & Keohler, M. (1998). Developing understanding of space and geometry in the primary grades. In E. Fennema & T. Romberg (Eds.), *Mathematics classrooms that promote understanding* (pp. 63–87). Mahwah, NJ: Erlbaum.

NCTM. (2000). *Principles and standards for school mathematics.* Reston, VA: NCTM.

Schifter, D., Bastable, V., & Russell, S. J. (2002). *Developing mathematical ideas: Measuring space in one, two, and three dimensions.* Parsippany, NJ: Dale Seymour Publications.

5

Data Analysis and Probability

Grades PreK–2

Informal comparing, classifying, and counting activities can provide the mathematical beginnings for developing young learners' understanding of data, analysis of data, and statistics. The types of activities needed and appropriate for kindergartners vary greatly from those for second graders; however, throughout the preK–2 years, students should pose questions to investigate, organize the responses, and create representations of their data. Through data investigations, teachers should encourage students to think clearly and to check new ideas against what they already know in order to develop concepts for making informed decisions.

As students' questions become more sophisticated and their data sets larger, their use of traditional representations should increase. By the end of the second grade, students should be able to organize and display their data through both graphical displays and numerical summaries. They should be using counts, tallies, tables, bar graphs, and line plots. The titles and labels for their displays should clearly identify what the data represent. As students work with numerical data, they should begin to sort out the meaning of the different numbers—those that represent values ("I have four people in my family") and those that represent how often a value occurs in a data set (frequency) ("Nine children have four people in their families"). They should discuss when conclusions about data from one population might or might not apply to data from another population. Considerations like these are the precursors to understanding the notion of inferences from samples (NCTM, 2000).

STRATEGY 21: *Encourage young children's collection, display, and organization of objects and data.*

NCTM Standard

Formulate questions that can be addressed with data and collect, organize, and display relevant data to answer them.

What Research and the NCTM Standards Say (NCTM, 2000)

The main purpose of collecting data is to answer questions when the answers are not immediately obvious. Students' natural inclination to ask questions must be nurtured. At the same time, teachers should help them develop ways to gather information to answer these questions so that they learn when and how to make decisions on the basis of data (Rosebery & Warren, 1992). As children enter school and their interests extend from their immediate surroundings to include other environments, they must learn how to keep track of multiple responses to their questions and those posed by others (Bright & Friel, 1998). Students also should begin to refine their questions to get the information they need.

Organizing data into categories should begin with informal sorting experiences, such as helping to put away groceries. These experiences and the conversations that accompany them focus children's attention on the attributes of objects and help develop an understanding of "things that go together," while building a vocabulary for describing attributes and for classifying according to criteria. Young students should continue activities that focus on attributes of objects and data so that by the second grade, they can sort and classify simultaneously, using more than one attribute.

Classroom Applications

Organizing data into categories can begin with everyday school experiences. Each day in Ms. Demarco's split kindergarten and first-grade classroom, she and her students take attendance and determine who is buying a school lunch. Students indicate whether they are having lunch from home or at school by clipping clothespins—labeled with their names—to a tall board that is divided into two columns and labeled Lunch from Home and Lunch from School. On Monday, by counting each clothespin in each category, her students are able to determine that ten students would have lunch from home and seven would have lunch at school. No one comments on the relationship between these data, the one clothespin left in the basket, and the number of students present. For the next few days, the totals are similar. However, on the fourth day, the school and home lunch counts are quite different. In this vignette (adapted from Russell, Schifter, & Bastable, 2002, Case 1), we listen in on the class discussion.

Todd exclaims, "We must be wrong because the numbers are too different." When Ms. Demarco asks him to explain, he clarifies, "All the other days we had ten and seven (home and school lunch count), and today we have twelve school lunches and only three lunches from home." A number of the other students also seem puzzled and the clothespins are recounted. Erick comments, "It's pizza today so I wanted to buy it. My pin is on the other side." Several children nod their heads in agreement, and Lindsay says, "Kids can change their minds. The number of pins depends on what the cook is making."

Ms. Demarco asks the class about the total number of clothespins used in the data gathering. Several students begin counting the pins by ones. Others add twelve and three. All reach a total of fifteen. Anita speaks up, "How could it be fifteen? There are eighteen kids in our class." Todd shouts, pointing to the basket, "Here are three pins. They're for the kids not here." Brunilda raises her hand. "Can the pins tell only one thing?" Ms. Demarco asks her what she means and Brunilda continues, "If the pins tell us how many school lunches and how many home lunches there are, can they tell us how many are at school, I mean at the same time?" The students discuss this idea and agree that the two totals always had to match; otherwise, someone wasn't eating lunch.

Ms. Demarco has provided a data collection experience that fosters children's natural inclination to ask questions. At the same time, she has structured the experience with the clothespins and her questions in ways that encourage, for example, the conjecture that the lunch count should match the attendance count.

Precautions and Possible Pitfalls

Students do not automatically refine their questions, consider alternative ways of collecting information, or choose the most appropriate way to organize and display data. Helping young students acquire such skills presents challenges for teachers: Left on their own students may be overwhelmed and wander off track; given too much assistance they may treat this as a computational exercise and lose sight of what the data represent (Konold & Higgins, 2003). Teachers need to design many activities that require students to think about the questions they are asking as they collect, display, and organize data.

Sources

Biehler, R. (1989). Educational perspectives on exploratory data analysis. In R. Morris (Ed.), *Studies in mathematics education, Vol. 7: The teaching of statistics* (pp. 185–201). Paris: UNESCO.

Bright, S. W., & Friel, S. N. (1998). Teach-stat: A model for professional development in data analysis and statistics for teachers K–6. In S. P. Lajoie (Ed.), *Reflections on statistics: Learning, teaching, and assessment in Grades K–12* (pp. 89–117). Mahwah, NJ: Erlbaum.

Konold, C., & Higgins, T. (2003). Reasoning about data. In J. Kilpatick, W. G. Martin, & D. Schifter (Eds.), *A research companion to* Principles and standards for school mathematics. Reston, VA: NCTM.

NCTM. (2000). *Principles and standards for school mathematics.* Reston, VA: NCTM.

Rosebery, A. S., & Warren, B. (1992). Appropriating scientific discourse: findings from language minority classrooms. *Journal of Learning Sciences, 2,* 61–94.

Russell, S. J., Schifter, D., & Bastable, V. (2002). *Developing mathematical ideas: Working with data.* Parsippany, NJ: Dale Seymour Publications.

STRATEGY 22: Encourage the idea in young children that data, graphs, and charts give information.

NCTM Standard

Select and use appropriate statistical methods to analyze data.

What Research and the NCTM Standards Say (NCTM, 2000)

Through their data investigations, young students should develop the idea that data, charts, and graphs give information. When data are displayed in an organized manner, class discussions should focus on what the graph or other representation conveys and whether the data help answer the specific questions that were posed (Konold & Higgins, 2003). Teachers should encourage students to compare parts of the data ("The same number of children have dogs as have cats") and make statements about the data as a whole ("Most students in the class have lost only two teeth").

By the end of Grade 2, students should begin to question inappropriate statements about data, as illustrated in this classroom conversation: Two students, interested in how many of their classmates watched a particular television show, surveyed only their friends and reported their results to the class. "You didn't ask me and I watched it!" one girl complained. Another student said, "Wait a minute, you didn't ask me and I didn't watch it. I bet most kids didn't watch it."

Classroom Applications

Appropriately organizing and representing data is essential to future inter-pretations. Ms. Kourounis's first-grade class has been working on a unit about data collection. Her students have used linking cubes, nametags, and stick-on notes to represent their data. The lesson today asks students to represent data from a survey done with the whole class. In this vignette (adapted from Russell, Schifter & Bastable, 2002, Case 8), we listen as Ms. Kourounis encour-ages her students to explore and develop appropriate representational strategies.

Ms. Kourounis has asked each student in the class to choose a pet, and then together she and the class have created a list that summarizes how many students choose a different kind of pet. Their list looks like this:

Figure 5.1

Dog	Cat	Fish	Bird	Guinea Pig
6	4	4	4	1

Ms. Kourounis then gives each student blank sheets of white paper and asks them to represent the pet data that had been collected in any way they choose, so long as it was clear and easy to understand. As she walks around the room, she notices that some students divide their papers into five boxes. Others make columns with a label on the top of each column, and still others make rows with the label at the beginning of each row. As the students finish, Ms. Kourounis asks them to write down what they noticed from their representations. Was there anything that surprised them?

The class meets to share their work and what they have noticed. Anita raises her hand. "I thought most kids would choose Dog because dogs are smart and fun to play with." Julius speaks up, "It was interesting that three of the choices have four kids choosing them." Ms. Kourounis asks, "What do we know about children in our class and their choices of a pet?" Lissette replies, "Most children in our class like Dog and only one kid likes Guinea Pig." Alexandra adds, "Cat, Fish, and Bird had the same number. Each was chosen by four kids."

In a previous lesson, many of Ms. Kourounis's students focused on making detailed pictures of each counted object. In this lesson, they focused on organizing and clearly communicating their data as information. Such a focus enabled them to both note interesting relationships—"Three of the choices have four kids choosing them"—and give informed answers to more general questions—"What do we know about children in our class and their choices of a pet?"

Precautions and Possible Pitfalls

Young children, in their displays of collected data, often produce detailed drawings of the events that gave rise to the data. While such drawings are developmentally appropriate for the preK student, older students should learn to see the numerical data they have collected as separate from the real-world event from which it has been abstracted—for example, using a label rather than a picture of a dog—and simultaneously see these abstracted numbers as providing information about the event. This process is more similar to that of impressionist painting than snapshot photography (Hancock, Kaput, & Goldsmith, 1992).

Sources

Hancock, C., Kaput, J. J., & Goldsmith, L. T. (1992). Authentic inquiry with data: Critical barriers to classroom implementation. *Educational Psychologist, 27,* 337–364.

Konold, C., & Higgins, T. (2003). Reasoning about data. In J. Kilpatrick, W. G. Martin, & D. Shifter (Eds.), *A research companion to* Principles and standards for school mathematics. Reston, VA: NCTM.

NCTM. (2000). *Principles and standards for school mathematics.* Reston, VA: NCTM.

Russell, S. J., Schifter, D., & Bastable, V. (2002). *Developing mathematical ideas: Working with data.* Parsippany, NJ: Dale Seymour Publications.

STRATEGY 23: Encourage young children's informal explorations of probability.

NCTM Standard

Understand and apply basic concepts of probability.

What Research and the NCTM Standards Say (NCTM, 2000)

 At this level, probability experiences should be informal, taking the form of answering questions about the likelihood of events, using vocabulary such as "more likely" or "less likely." Young students enjoy thinking about impossible events and often encounter them in the books they are learning to read. Questions about more likely and less likely events should come from the students' experiences, and the answers will often depend on the community and its location (Konold, 1989). During the winter, the question "Is it likely to snow tomorrow?" has quite different answers in Toronto and San Diego.

Teachers should address the beginnings of probability through informal activities with spinners or number cubes that reinforce conceptions in other Standards, primarily Numbers and Operations. For example, as students repeatedly toss two dice or number cubes and add the results of each toss, they may begin to keep track of the results. They will realize that a sum of 1 is impossible, that a sum of 2 or 12 is rare, and that the sums 6, 7, and 8 are fairly common. Through discussion, they may realize that their observations have something to do with the number of ways to get a particular sum from two dice, but the exact calculation of the probabilities should occur in higher grades.

Classroom Applications

Teachers can begin an introduction of probability concepts to young children by involving them in experiments where they can learn that, for example, some outcomes are more likely than others. In this vignette (adapted from Burns & Tank, 1988, Experiments With Spinners), we listen in as Ms. Jimenez teaches such a unit on probability. Ms. Jimenez has made several spinners for her second graders to use. Each spinner has a yellow face, half of which was devoted to the number 3, with the other half divided into two equal segments, numbered 1 and 2.

Figure 5.2

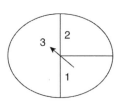

Ms. Jimenez models for the class how the spinners work and asks her students to make some predictions. Several students think that 3 will come up first since it takes up more space than the other numbers.

Ms. Jimenez gives directions for the experiment. Each group is to have a spinner and they are to record their spins, beginning on the bottom row and working up, on a record sheet with three columns—labeled with the numbers 1, 2, and 3—and ten rows.

	1	2	3
10th occurrence			x
⋮			
2nd occurrence	x		x
1st occurrence	x	x	x

The number that reaches the top row first is said to have *won*. She models how this is to be done—and she writes 1, 2, 3 on the chalkboard, ruling lines to define a space under each number. She says, "When you've completed your experiment, tape your sheet under the number that reached the top of the column." Derrick comments, "They'll all be under the 3."

After the students finish the experiment and post their results, the class gathers for a discussion. Ms. Jimenez takes one of the student records— one that has five 1s, four 2s, and ten 3s,—and notes, "This record shows results that look like what the spinner should do. Let me explain why. The 3s are at the top, and, as most of you said, it makes sense for the threes to finish first. The 3s came up ten times. The 1 and 2 together came up about as many times, nine times altogether. What can you say about that?" Melanie raises her hand. "Because the 1 and 2 take up as much space as the 3 does." Others agree.

Ms. Jimenez has provided an opportunity for her students to informally explore notions of chance and randomness. Such activities also provide opportunities for students to categorize, organize, and analyze experimental data.

Precautions and Possible Pitfalls

Although young children do not have a complete understanding of probability ratios—that is, it is the magnitude of the ratio that determines likelihood—they do have notions of chance or randomness (Shaughnessy, 2003). These notions can serve as a basis for challenging and deepening students' conceptions and misconceptions about chance. However, for challenges to be effective, students need the experience of organizing and analyzing actual data and making their own conjectures about chance.

Sources

Burns, M., & Tank, B. (1988). *A collection of math lessons: From Grades 1 through 3.* Sausalito, CA: Math Solution Publications.

Konold, C. (1989). Informal conceptions of probability. *Cognition and Instruction,* 6, 59–98.

NCTM. (2000). *Principles and standards for school mathematics.* Reston, VA: NCTM.

Shaughnessy, J. M. (2003). Research on students' understandings of probability. In J. Kilpatrick, W. G. Martin, & D. Shifter (Eds.), *A research companion to Principles and standards for school mathematics.* Reston, VA: NCTM.

Grades 3–5

In prekindergarten through Grade 2, students will have learned that data can give them information about aspects of their world. They should know how to organize and represent data sets and be able to notice individual aspects of the data—where their own data are on the graph, for instance, or what value occurs most frequently in the data set. In Grades 3–5, students should move toward seeing a set of data as a whole, describing its shape, and using statistical characteristics of the data such as range and measures of center to compare data sets. Much of this work emphasizes the comparison of related data sets. As students learn to describe the similarities and differences between data sets, they will have an opportunity to develop clear descriptions of the data and to formulate conclusions and arguments based on the data. They should consider how the data sets they collect are samples from larger populations and should learn how to use language and symbols to describe simple situations involving probability (NCTM, 2000).

STRATEGY 24: *Encourage students to explore questions they find personally relevant and that can be addressed by data collection and analysis.*

NCTM Standard

Formulate questions that can be addressed with data and collect, organize, and display relevant data to answer them.

What Research and the NCTM Standards Say (NCTM, 2000)

At these grade levels, students should pose questions about themselves and their environment, issues in their school or community, and content they are studying in different subject areas: How do fourth graders spend their time after school? Do automobiles stop at the stop signs in our neighborhood? How can the amount of water used for common daily activities be decreased? Once a question is posed, students can develop a plan to collect information to address the question. They may collect their own data, use data already collected by their school or town, or use other existing data sets such as the census or weather data accessible on the Internet to examine particular questions. If students collect their own data, they need to decide whether it is appropriate to conduct a survey or to use observations or measurements. As part of their plan, they often need to refine their question and to consider aspects of data collection such as how to word questions, whom to ask, what and when to observe, what and how to measure, and how to record their data (Jacobs, 1999; Schwartz et al., 1998). When they use existing data, they still need to consider and evaluate the ways in which the data were collected.

Classroom Applications

Ms. Ortiz has been working with her fifth graders on the significance of asking questions for the purpose of collecting data. In this vignette (adapted from Russell, Schifter, & Bastable, 2002, Case 5), we listen as Ms. Ortiz asks her students to brainstorm some questions they would like to research.

Ms. Ortiz's students talk in small groups as she walks around and listens. John's group wants to find out if kids in fifth and sixth grade played sports. His group had come up with the question "How many sports do you play?" Ms. Ortiz asks, "What do you mean by a sport?" John replies, "Anything you play?" Ms. Ortiz asks whether rope jumping is a sport. The group looks puzzled and John says, "No, it has to be in a group." Ms. Ortiz says, "What about tennis?" The group looks unsure.

The next group wants to ask about how many languages children spoke. Their question was "Do you speak more than one language?" Ms. Ortiz asks them, "How do we know when someone *speaks* another language? For example, suppose you know how to say *Where is the bathroom?* in French, and that's all you know. Is that *speaking French*? Deana replies, "No. We mean speaking fluently." Ms. Ortiz challenges the group to think about the meaning of fluency. After some discussion, the group comes up with this definition: *You need to know more than half the total of words in that language, and you need to know and understand what you are saying in a conversation.*

Another group wants to find out how many times fifth graders in their class had moved. Their original question had been "How many times did you move in the last ten years?" Craig, however, has objected saying, "Some of the kids in the fifth grade aren't ten yet," and Sofia has suggested, "Let's ask how many times did you move in your life." Ms. Ortiz asks, "What do you mean by *moving*? Craig replies, "Going from one place to another," and Charlene adds, "From state to state." Ms. Ortiz asks about moving from one side of town to another. The students think about this for a moment, and Sofia says, "Yeah! Even from the same neighborhood, like John did this year. Do we count moving to camp if you take your stuff and spend two months at camp? My brother just went to college. I am in his room now with his TV . . . Wait! Is this *moving*?"

Ms. Ortiz has provided an opportunity for her students to refine their understandings of questions that might be posed in a survey. An essential component of this experience was Ms. Ortiz's probing of students' preconceptions and definitions. As her students think about how they might answer a question, they find that the wording of the questions matters.

Precautions and Possible Pitfalls

As children formulate statistical questions prior to collecting and analyzing data, they must learn ways of posing and refining such questions that support reasonable and relevant data collection. For instance, when students are asked to think about how they might answer a proposed question, they discover not only the range of different responses but that multiple and unwanted interpretations of a question may be possible (Konold & Higgins, 2003). Formulating questions that are appropriate for data collection and analysis is a difficult skill to acquire and needs to be developed through experience, reflection, and teacher guidance.

Sources

Jacobs, V. R. (1999). How do students think about statistical sampling before instruction? *Mathematics Teaching in the Middle School, 5,* 240–246, 263.

Konold, C., & Higgins, T. (2003). Reasoning about data. In J. Kilpatrick, W. G. Martin, & D. Shifter (Eds.), *A research companion to* Principles and standards for school mathematics. Reston, VA: NCTM.

NCTM .(2000). *Principles and standards for school mathematics.* Reston, VA: NCTM.

Russell, S. J., Schifter, D., & Bastable, V. (2002). *Developing mathematical ideas: Working with data.* Parsippany, NJ: Dale Seymour Publications.

Schwartz, D. L., Goldman, S. R., Vye, N. J., & Barron, B. J. (1998). Aligning everyday and mathematical reasoning: The case of sampling assumptions. In S. P. Lajoie (Ed.), *Reflections on statistics: Learning, teaching, and assessment in Grades K–12* (pp. 233–273). Mahwah, NJ: Erlbaum.

STRATEGY 25: *Encourage students to become more precise in their mathematical descriptions of data.*

NCTM Standard

Select and use appropriate statistical methods to analyze data.

What Research and the NCTM Standards Say (NCTM, 2000)

In prekindergarten through Grade 2, students are often most interested in individual pieces of data, especially their own, or which value is "the most" on a graph. A reasonable objective for upper elementary and middle-grades students is that they begin to regard a set of data as a whole that can be described as a set and compared to other data sets (Konold & Higgins, 2003). Noting the similarities and differences between two data sets requires students to become more precise in their descriptions of the data. In this context, students gradually develop the idea of a "typical," or average, value. Building on their informal understanding of "the most" and "the middle," students can learn about three measures of center—mode, median, and, informally, the mean. Students need to learn more than simply how to identify the mode or median in a data set. They need to build an understanding of what, for example, the median tells them about the data, and they need to see this value in the context of other characteristics of the data.

Classroom Applications

Teachers can encourage their students to focus more precisely on the shape of the data—where data are concentrated or clumped, values for which there are no data, or data points that appear to have unusual values—and how the data are spread across the range of values. Ms. Brisbane's third-grade class has decided on the following survey question:

"What is your usual bedtime on a school night—When is 'lights out'?"

Then, with class lists in hand, her students have visited the twenty kindergartens through fifth-grade classrooms in their school. Her students also have spent some time discussing how to organize the data—they have settled on line plots. In this vignette (adapted from Russell, Schifter, & Bastable, 2002, Case 19), we listen in as Ms. Brisbane's students are comparing the data from different-age children.

Ms. Brisbane has just asked the class what they noticed. Portia raises her hand. "For the first and second grade, eight-thirty is the longest one on the paper." Maria adds, "In kindergarten, the highest is at eight o'clock and then it just goes up a half an hour. In the first grade, it's eight-thirty and then goes up another half an hour, and it's nine o'clock for third and fourth grade." Ms Brisbane asks, "Does anybody remember the mathematical term for the one that's highest?" The students are momentarily quiet and then Tamara says, "Mode." Ms. Brisbane says, "Mode. So you're looking at the mode. So what was the pattern you noticed, Maria?" Maria replies, "It just goes up by half an hour."

Ms. Brisbane asks if there was anything else the class noticed when they compared the data across the grades. Ileana raises her hand. "I noticed that in first and second, there is a wider span of bedtimes than in kindergarten, third and fourth, and fifth grade." Ms. Brisbane replies, "So you're calling it the span, or in other words, the range. What is the range in kindergarten?" Ileana answers, "Six to ten-thirty—four and a half hours—and the range in first and second is five hours." Ms. Brisbane asks Ileana about the ranges at the other grade level, and Ileana notes that at third and fourth, it is three and a half hours and at fifth it is three hours and forty-five minutes. Ms. Brisbane ask, "So what are you saying about the ranges?" Ileana replies, "The ranges are all different, and if you look at how it's different, the first and second graders have a longer range."

While the data set does seem to lend itself to discussions of mode and range, it is Ms. Brisbane who builds on the informal observations of her students so as to encourage them to become more precise in their mathematical descriptions of data. Maria's "highest" becomes *mode* and Ileana's "span" becomes *range.*

Precautions and Possible Pitfalls

Children often have difficulty in making a conceptual leap from seeing data as a grouping of individuals each with its own attributes to seeing data as an aggregate with attributes—such as the mode or range—that are not evident in any individual member. Even when teachers explicitly encourage the computation and use of terms such as mode or range to characterize data, students find it difficult to generalize beyond the particulars of a single observation. Thus, most researchers now recommend that in the elementary grades, understanding—for example, helping children to connect their common understandings of terms such mode and range with those used in the mathematics classroom—and appropriate application should be emphasized prior to, for instance, standard computations of the mean (Konold & Higgins, 2003).

Sources

Konold, C., & Higgins, T. (2003). Reasoning about data. In J. Kilpatrick, W. G. Martin, & D. Shifter (Eds.), *A research companion to* Principles and standards for school mathematics. Reston, VA: NCTM.

NCTM. (2000). *Principles and standards for school mathematics.* Reston, VA: NCTM.

Russell, S. J., Schifter, D., & Bastable, V. (2002). *Developing mathematical ideas: Working with data.* Parsippany, NJ: Dale Seymour Publications.

 STRATEGY 26: Encourage students to explore and evaluate issues of representativeness and inference.

NCTM Standard

 Develop and evaluate inferences and predictions that are based on data.

What Research and the NCTM Standards Say (NCTM, 2000)

Data can be used for developing arguments that are based on evidence and for continued problem posing. As students discuss data gathered to address a particular question, they should begin to distinguish between what the data show and what might account for the results (Konold & Higgins, 2003). Students can be encouraged to develop conjectures, show how these are based on the data, consider alternative explanations, and design further studies to examine their conjectures.

With appropriate experiences, students should begin to understand that many data sets are samples of larger populations. They can look at several samples drawn from the same population; such as different classrooms in their school, or compare statistics about their own sample to known parameters for a larger population; for example, how the median family size for their class compares with the median family size reported for their town. They can think about the issues that affect the representativeness of a sample—how well it represents the population from which it is drawn—and begin to notice how samples from the same population can vary.

Classroom Applications

Teachers can provide suitable contexts for students in Grades 3–5 to explore issues of representativeness and inference. Ms. Ko has asked her fourth-grade students to measure their own heights and then collect student heights from a first-grade classroom. Her students have met in groups to plan how they are going to represent these two sets of data, and they have created their representations. In this vignette (adapted from Russell, Schifter, & Bastable, as cited in CBMS, 2001, pp. 89–90), we listen as Ms. Ko's students, with their representations of the data posted in front of the room, discuss what they see in the data.

Rosa notes, "First graders are a lot smaller. The biggest first grader is fifty-four inches." Lee adds, "A lot of first graders are near the heights of the smallest fourth graders. Not many are as tall as an average fourth grader in our class. Most fourth graders are fifty-seven or fifty-eight inches." Ms. Ko asks, "Does that tell you something you could say generally about all first graders and all fourth graders?" A number of the other fourth graders seem unsure.

Ms. Ko continues, "Can you give me a number that says how much taller a fourth grader is than a first grader, thinking about all the different ways you've thought about first-grader heights and fourth-grader heights?" Jeanette raises her hand. "Ten inches, because the tallest fourth grader is sixty-four inches and the tallest first grader is fifty-four inches." Karolyn speaks up, "I think a first grader is about five inches smaller than a fourth grader. I found the median of fourth graders and first graders and I just subtracted." Tamara nods and adds, "Five or four inches because the average first grader, the most common height, is fifty-three inches, and the average fourth grader is fifty-eight inches or fifty-seven inches." Roberto speaks up, "I think to find the range between the first and fourth graders we need data from all the fourth-grade classes and the first-grade classes."

Ms. Ko's question "Can you give me a number that says how much taller a fourth grader is than a first grader?" builds on conjectures of her students, encouraging them to see further into their data. Roberto's response potentially provides an opportunity to discuss issues surrounding the representativeness of the students' single fourth-grade/first-grade sample.

Precautions and Possible Pitfalls

The ideal *average* that many elementary children appear to have in mind is that which is also the mode and which occurs, roughly, midway between the two extremes of range (Konold & Higgins, 2003). Thus, it is not unusual for children to use the mode (or the midrange) inappropriately. For instance, students who conceive of averages only in terms of the mode may be unable to solve a problem that asks them to price nine bags of potato chips for which the average or usual price is $1.38 without any of the individual prices being $1.38 (Mokros & Russell, 1995). Many researchers (Bakker, 2001; Cobb, 1999; Mokros & Russell, 1995) have suggested that formal computations of the mean and median should be preceded by and based on appropriate analytical experiences with the mode and midrange.

Sources

Bakker, A. (2001). Historical and didactical phenomenology of the average values. In P. Radelet-de Grave (Ed.), *Proceedings of the conference on history and epsitemology in mathematics education* (Vol. 1, pp. 91–106). Louvain-la-Neuve & Leuven, Belgium: Catholic Universities of Louvain-la-Neuve & Leuven.

CBMS. (2001). *Issues in mathematics education: The mathematical education of teachers,* Vol. 11. Washington, DC: American Mathematical Society.

Cobb, P. (1999). Individual and collective mathematical development: The case of statistical data analysis. *Mathematical Thinking and Learning, 1,* 5–43.

Konold, C., & Higgins, T. (2003). Reasoning about data. In J. Kilpatrick, W. G. Martin, & D. Shifter (Eds.), *A research companion to* Principles and standards for school mathematics. Reston, VA: NCTM.

Mokros, J., & Russell, S. (1995). Children's concepts of average and representativeness. *Journal for Research in Mathematics Education, 26,* 20–39.

NCTM. (2000). *Principles and standards for school mathematics.* Reston, VA: NCTM.

STRATEGY 27: Encourage students' exploration and quantification of simple probabilistic events.

NCTM Standard

Understand and apply basic concepts of probability.

What Research and the NCTM Standards Say (NCTM, 2000)

 Students in Grades 3–5 should begin to learn about probability as a measurement of the likelihood of events (Shaughnessy, 2003). In previous grades, they will have begun to describe events as certain, likely, or impossible, but now they can begin to learn how to quantify likelihood. For instance, what is the likelihood of seeing a commercial when you turn on the television? To estimate this probability, students could collect data about the number of minutes of commercials in an hour.

Students should also explore probability through experiments that have only a few outcomes, such as using game spinners with certain portions shaded and considering how likely it is that the spinner will land on a particular color. They should come to understand and use 0 to represent the probability of an impossible event and 1 to represent the probability of a certain event, and they should use common fractions to represent the probability of events that are neither certain nor impossible. Through these experiences, students encounter the idea that although they cannot determine an individual outcome, such as which color the spinner will land on next, they can predict the frequency of various outcomes.

Classroom Applications

Mr. Hilburn has been working on probability for a few days with his fifth graders. He began by asking his students to decide whether a coin-tossing game he presented was fair or not. He found that although most of his students did consider the possible outcomes, they did not analyze the way those outcomes could be obtained. That is, they thought that when you tossed two coins, it was equally likely to get two heads, two tails, or a head and a tail. Mr. Hilburn has designed a dice-tossing game, and today he has asked his student to determine whether this game is fair:

Two Players

Choose one player to be "even" and the other to be "odd."

Throw two dice.

Add the numbers on the two faces.

If the sum is even, the even player gets 1 point.

If the sum is odd, the odd player gets 1 point.

Mr. Hilburn's students pair off and work on the problem. Some play the game first, recording their results, as a means of investigating the question. Others try to analyze the games based on the possible outcomes. After they have played the game or worked on their analyses for a while, Mr. Hilburn directs the students to stop, to open their notebooks, and to write in their notebooks what they think about the fairness of the two games.

In this vignette (adapted from NCTM, 1991, Vignette 2.3), we listen in as Mr. Hilburn opens the fairness of the game to a whole-class discussion. Based on what he has observed, Mr. Hilburn calls on Sandy and Peter. Sandy explains that they had figured out the game was unfair and that they didn't even need to play it. Peter provides their reasoning, "There are six even sums possible—two, four, six, eight, ten, and twelve—but only five odd ones—three, five, seven, nine, and eleven. So the game is unfair to the person who gets points for the odd sums."

Mr. Hilburn asks the class what they think. Some shake their heads and some nod. "Rick," he inquires. Rick answers, "It doesn't make sense to me, Mr. Hilburn. I think that there's more ways to get some of those numbers, like there's two ways to get a three. But there is only one way to get a two." A number of the students look puzzled, and Mr. Hilburn asks Rick to explain what he means. Rick explains, "Well, you could get a *one* on one die and a *two* on the other, or you could get a *two* on the first die and a *one* on the other. That's two different ways." Sara speaks up, "But how are those different? One plus two equals the same thing as two plus one!" Mr. Hilburn asks, "What do you think, Marc?" After a moment Marc says, "But they are different dice, so it is not the same."

    Mr. Hilburn has provided a context that encourages his students' exploration and quantification of a probabilistic event. Based on his classroom observations, he asks Sandy and Peter to present their solution because they, although incorrect, have attempted to quantify the probabilities in the game. He then asks for comments from Rick and Marc as he has reason to believe that they have critical and additional insights. Finally, Mr. Hilburn, so as to encourage further quantification and exploration, reassigns the coin-tossing game for homework:

Three Players

One player is *heads*, one player is *tails*, and one player is *mixed*.

Toss two coins.

If the result is two heads, the *heads* player gets 1 point.

If the result is two tails, the *tails* player gets 1 point.

If the result is one head and one tail, the *mixed* player gets 1 point.

He thinks that once the students see that the mixed player gets about twice as many points as the other players, they will notice what is going on.

Precautions and Possible Pitfalls

 Although children have hunches and intuitions about probability, many are weak on the concept of sample space. They are often unsure what the outcomes of a probability experiment are and how to assign probabilities to these outcomes. For example, in the tossing of two dice, children may argue that there are 11 possibilities (the sums),

15 possibilities (the number pairs without considering order), or 36 possibilities (the ordered number pairs). Children need hands-on activities to test their conjectures and opportunities to carefully discuss, with their peers, the set of all possible outcomes for a probability experiment or a sampling activity (Shaughnessy, 2003).

Sources

NCTM. (1991). *Professional standards for teaching mathematics.* Reston, VA: NCTM.

NCTM. (2000). *Principles and standards for school mathematics.* Reston, VA: NCTM.

Shaughnessy, J. M. (2003). Research on students' understandings of probability. In J. Kilpatrick, W. G. Martin, & D. Shifter (Eds.), *A research companion to Principles and standards for school mathematics.* Reston, VA: NCTM.

6

Problem Solving

Grades PreK–2

Problem solving is a hallmark of mathematical activity and a major means of developing mathematical knowledge. It is finding a way to reach a goal that is not immediately attainable. Problem solving is natural to young children because the world is new to them, and they exhibit curiosity, intelligence, and flexibility as they face new situations. The challenge at this level is to build on children's innate problem-solving inclinations and to preserve and encourage a disposition that values problem solving. Teachers should encourage students to use the new mathematics they are learning to develop a broad range of problem-solving strategies, to pose and formulate challenging problems, and to learn to monitor and reflect on their own ideas in solving problems (NCTM, 2000).

 STRATEGY 28: *Encourage young children to ask mathematical questions and to identify essential mathematical information.*

NCTM Standard

 What should problem solving look like in Grades PreK through 2?

What Research and the NCTM Standards Say (NCTM, 2000)

Problem solving in the early years should involve a variety of contexts, from problems related to daily routines to mathematical situations arising from stories (Hong, 1999; Warfield & Yttri, 1999). Students in the same classroom are likely to have very different mathematical understandings and skills; the same situation that is a problem for one student may elicit an automatic response from another. For instance, the question "How many books would there be on the shelf if Marita put six books on it and Al put three more on it?" may not be a problem for the student who knows the basic number combination 6 and 3 and its connection with the question. For the student who has not yet learned the number combination and may not yet know how to represent the task symbolically, this problem presents an opportunity to learn the skills and dispositions needed to solve similar problems.

Classroom Applications

Posing problems is a mathematical disposition teachers should encourage and develop. Through asking questions and identifying essential mathematical information, students can learn to effectively organize their thoughts and identify essential mathematical information. Ms. Lubick's first graders have been constructing patterns with pattern blocks. In this vignette (adapted from NCTM, 2000, p. 117), we listen in as Lei, one of Ms. Lubick's students, decides that she "wants to know all the ways to cover a yellow hexagon with other pattern blocks."

Figure 6.1

At first, Lei works with the pattern blocks using fairly unstructured trial and error. Gradually, however, she becomes more methodical and places her various arrangements in rows. Lei then organizes these arrangements by the number of blocks used and begins predicting which attempts would be transformations of other arrangements even before she completes a new arrangement.

Figure 6.2

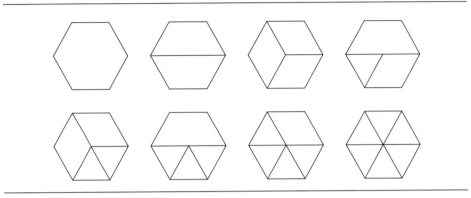

Kyle, who has been watching Lei, tells Ms. Lubick and Lei that he is certain that he can find more coverings for the hexagon than Lei has found. Other students join the discussions between Lei and Jack. When this activity creates a great demand for "turns" with the pattern blocks, Ms. Lubick takes advantage of their interest by having students discuss how they would know when an arrangement of blocks was a duplicate and how they might keep a written record of their work.

Ms. Lubick has structured an opportunity for her students to pose and seek solutions to a variety of questions central to problem solving. For example, what distinguishes a *new* covering of the hexagon? How will Lei or Jack know they have found all the coverings of a hexagon, and how might they and fellow students keep a written record of their work?

Precautions and Possible Pitfalls

While word problems can be designed to provide contexts for young children to develop problem-solving skills, they are often little more than camouflaged skill practice. Thus, problem solving can become formulaic; a matter of remembering which numbers to substitute for which words. Contextualized problems, such as the above, are designed to deepen young children's mathematics skills, to anticipate and develop their geometric and numeric modeling of the real world, and to involve them in searching for patterns, constructing models, and proposing and proving conjectures (Fosnot & Dolk, 2001),

Sources

Fosnot, C. T., and Dolk, M. (2001). *Young mathematicians at work: Constructing early number sense, addition and subtraction.* Portsmouth, NH: Heinemann.

Hong, H. (1999). The development of informal counting, number, and arithmetic skills and concepts. In J. V. Copley (Ed.), *Mathematics in the early years* (pp. 162–168). Reston, VA: NCTM.

NCTM. (2000). *Principles and standards for school mathematics*. Reston, VA: NCTM.

Warfield, J., & Yttri, M. J. (1999). The development of informal counting, number, and arithmetic skills and concepts. In J. V. Copley (Ed.), *Mathematics in the early years* (pp. 103–111). Reston, VA: NCTM.

STRATEGY 29: *Assess young children's abilities to solve problems through examination of student work and conversations.*

NCTM Standard

What should be the teacher's role in developing problem solving in Grades PreK through 2?

What Research and the NCTM Standards Say (NCTM, 2000)

The decisions that teachers make about problem-solving opportunities influence the depth and breadth of students' mathematics learning. Teachers must be clear about the mathematics they want their students to accomplish as they structure situations that are both problematic and attainable for a wide range of students. Teachers make important decisions about when to probe, when to give feedback that affirms what is correct and identifies what is incorrect, when to withhold comments and plan similar tasks, and when to use class discussions to advance the students' mathematical thinking. By allowing time for thinking, believing that young students can solve problems, listening carefully to their explanations, and structuring an environment that values the work that students do, teachers promote problem solving and help students make their strategies explicit.

Teachers must make certain that problem solving is not reserved for older students or those who have "got the basics." Young students can engage in substantive problem solving and in doing so develop basic skills, higher-order-thinking skills, and problem-solving strategies (Cobb et al., 1991; Trafton & Hartman, 1997).

Classroom Applications

Assessing students' abilities to solve problems is more difficult than evaluating computational skills. However, it is imperative that teachers gather evidence in a variety of ways—for instance, through students' work and conversations—and use that information to plan how to help individual students in a whole-class context. Knowing students' interests allows teachers to formulate problems that extend the mathematical thinking of some students and that also reinforce the concepts learned by other students who have not yet reached the same understandings. The following two short vignettes (adapted from NCTM, 2000, p. 120) illustrate how conversations with students can give teachers useful information about students' thinking.

Katie, a kindergarten student, said that her sister in third grade had taught her to multiply. "Give me a problem," she said. Her teacher, Ms. Zamora, asked, "How much is three times four?" There was a long pause before Katie replied, "Twelve!" When Ms. Zamora asked how she knew, Katie responded, "I counted ducks in my head—three groups with four ducks."

Luis, a second grader, demonstrated fluency with composing and decomposing numbers when he announced that he could figure out multiplication. His teacher, Mr. Batista, asked, "Can you tell me four times seven?" Luis was quiet for a few moments, and then he gave the answer 28. When Mr. Batista asked how he got 28, Luis replied, "Seven plus three is ten, and four more is fourteen; six more is twenty and one more is twenty-one; seven more is twenty-eight."

Both Luis and Katie appear to be demonstrating an additive understanding of multiplication. Katie, while counting the ducks in each group, was also exhibiting an interest in, and readiness for, mathematics that is traditionally a focus in the higher grades. Luis's approach appears to include a far more sophisticated use of number relationships. He added $7 + 7 + 7 + 7$ mentally by breaking the sevens into parts to complete tens along the way:

$$
\begin{aligned}
7 + 7 &= (7 + 3) + 4 \\
&= 10 + 4 \\
&= 14 \\
14 + 7 &= (14 + 6) + 1 \\
&= 20 + 1 \\
&= 21 \\
21 + 7 &= 28
\end{aligned}
$$

In addition to displaying an additive understanding of multiplication, both Katie and Luis are providing their teachers indications of how they use and understand numbers. Luis uses the place value structure of our number system to compute his answer. Katie appears to envision each number as a *duck* and counts rather than adds three groups of four *ducks*. However, if Ms. Zamora had questioned further, she might have found that Katie is actually skip-counting by fours—that is, 4, 8, 12 .

Precautions and Possible Pitfalls

When demonstrating and discussing problem-solving strategies, teachers should take into account children's different learning rates. Teachers should give children sufficient time to reflect on, explain, and justify their answers so that problem solving both leads to and provides confirmation of their understanding of mathematics concepts. If time is taken for modeling and discussion, all children can develop the necessary understandings (Posamentier, Hartman, & Kaiser, 1998).

Sources

Cobb, P., Wood, T., Yackel, E., Nicholls, J., Wheatley, G., Trigatti, B., & Perlwitz, M. (1991). Assessment of a problem-centered second-grade mathematics project. *Journal for Research in Mathematics Education, 22,* 3–29.

NCTM. (2000). *Principles and standards for school mathematics.* Reston, VA: NCTM.

Posamentier, A. S., Hartman, H. J., & Kaiser, C. (1998). *Tips for the mathematics teacher: Research-based strategies to help students learn.* Thousand Oaks, CA: Corwin Press.

Trafton, P. R., & Hartman, C. L. (1997). Developing number sense and computational strategies in problem-centered classrooms. *Teaching Children Mathematics, 4,* 230–233.

Grades 3–5

Problem solving is the cornerstone of school mathematics. Without the ability to solve problems, the usefulness and power of mathematical ideas, knowledge, and skills are severely limited. Students who can efficiently and accurately multiply but who cannot identify situations that call for multiplication are not well prepared. Students who can both develop and carry out a plan to solve a mathematical problem are exhibiting knowledge that is much deeper and more useful than simply carrying out a computation. Unless students can solve problems, the facts, concepts, and procedures they know are of little use. The goal of school mathematics should be for all students to become increasingly able and willing to engage with and solve problems.

Problem solving is also important because it can serve as a vehicle for learning new mathematical ideas and skills (Schroeder & Lester, 1989). A problem-centered approach to teaching mathematics uses interesting and well-selected problems to launch mathematical lessons and engage students. In this way, new ideas, techniques, and mathematical relationships emerge and become the focus of discussion. Good problems can inspire the exploration of important mathematical ideas, nurture persistence, and reinforce the need to understand and use various strategies, mathematical properties, and relationships (NCTM, 2000).

 STRATEGY 30: Encourage students' development and application of problem-solving strategies.

NCTM Standard

 What should problem solving look like in Grades 3 through 5?

What Research and the NCTM Standards Say (NCTM, 2000)

Students in Grades 3–5 should have frequent experiences with problems that interest, challenge, and engage them in thinking about important mathematics. Problem solving is not a distinct topic but a process that should permeate the study of mathematics and provide a context in which concepts and skills are learned (Hiebert et al., 1996). Good problems and problem-solving tasks encourage reflection and communication and can emerge from the students' environment or from purely mathematical contexts. They generally serve multiple purposes, such as challenging students to develop and apply strategies, introducing them to new concepts, and providing a context for using skills. Good problems should lead somewhere, mathematically.

Classroom Applications

 Mr. Cannavo has been thinking about how to help his fourth graders learn about multiplicative factors and, concurrently, how to encourage them in their development and application of problem-solving strategies. He realizes

that learning about multiplicative factors and developing problem-solving strategies entails developing concepts, procedures, and skills and has asked his students to work on the following problem-solving task:

Show all the rectangular regions you can make using 24 tiles (1-inch squares). You need to use all the tiles. Count and keep a record of the area and perimeter of each rectangle and then look for and describe any relationships you notice.

In this vignette (adapted from NCTM, 2000, pp. 183–184), we listen in as Mr. Cannavo's students begin to discuss their results.

Mr. Cannavo asks if anyone has constructed a rectangle with a length of 1, of 2, of 3, and so on, and organizes their answers in a chart:

Length (L) (units)	Width (W) (units)	Area (A) (sq. units)	Perimeter (P) (units)
1	24	24	50
2	12	24	28
3	8	24	22
4	6	24	20
6	4	24	20
8	3	24	22
12	2	24	28
24	1	24	50

He then asks the class if they see any mathematical relationships. Lisa raises her hand and notes that the numbers in the first two columns of any row can be multiplied to get 24 (the area). Mr. Cannavo writes $L \times W = 24$ on the white board and then emphasizes that one can use the term *factors of 24* as another way, in addition to length and width, to describe the numbers in the first two columns.

Chris and Heather note that as the numbers for one dimension increased (for example, the length), those for the other dimension decreased, and Rachael notes that the perimeters were always even. Carolyn raises her hand and asks if the rectangles at the bottom of the chart were the same as the ones at the top, just turned different ways. This observation prompts Mr. Cannavo to remind his students that the class had talked about this idea as a property of multiplication—the commutative property—and as congruence of rectangular figures.

The "24 tiles" problem provides opportunities for Mr. Cannavo's students to develop and apply problem-solving strategies, and, concurrently, to practice their computational skills. For instance, the problem provides opportunities for the class and Mr. Cannavo to model and discuss different aspects of problem solving—building all the rectangles, organizing the data, looking for patterns, and making and justifying conjectures. Concurrently, Mr. Cannavo's students are asked to reflect on the relationship between area—length times width equals area—and perimeter, to model the commutative property of multiplication, to use a particular mathematics vocabulary (*factor* and *multiple*), to record data in an organized way, and to review basic number combinations.

Precautions and Possible Pitfalls

The questions and comments generated by children in their solving of mathematical problems can often seem unpolished and may even sound inaccurate. Consequently, teachers may attempt to revoice or otherwise correct such discourse. While such revoicing has a place in the classroom—for example, Mr. Cannavo's emphasis on *factors of 24*—teachers need to provide space for and respect children's efforts to communicate their questions, conjectures, or strategies. There may be times, for example, when questions and comments generated by the students themselves are more fully understood by their peers than questions or comments provided to them by the teacher (Posamentier, Hartman, & Kaiser, 1998).

Sources

Hiebert, J., Carpenter, T. P., Fennema, E., Fuson, K., Human, P., Murray, H., Olivier, A., & Wearne, D. (1996). Problem solving as a basis for reform in curriculum and instruction: The case of mathematics. *Educational Researcher, 25*, 12–21.

NCTM. (2000). *Principles and standards for school mathematics.* Reston, VA: NCTM.

Posamentier, A. S., Hartman, H. J., & Kaiser, C. (1998). *Tips for the mathematics teacher: Research-based strategies to help students learn.* Thousand Oaks, CA: Corwin Press.

Schroeder, T. L., & Lester, F. K. (1989). Developing understanding in mathematics via problem solving. In P. R. Trafton (Ed.), *New directions for elementary school mathematics* (pp. 31–42). Reston, VA: NCTM.

STRATEGY 31: *Select rich, appropriate, and challenging problems and orchestrate their use.*

NCTM Standard

What should be the teacher's role in developing problem solving in Grades 3 through 5?

What Research and the NCTM Standards Say (NCTM, 2000)

Teachers can help students become problem solvers by selecting rich and appropriate problems, orchestrating their use, and assessing students' understanding and use of strategies. Students are more likely to develop confidence and self-assurance as problem solvers in classrooms where they play a role in establishing the classroom norms and where everyone's ideas are respected and valued (Schoenfeld, 1992). These attitudes are essential if students are expected to make sense of mathematics and to take intellectual risks by raising questions, formulating conjectures, and offering mathematical arguments. Since good problems challenge students to think, students will often struggle to arrive at solutions. It is the teacher's responsibility to know when students need assistance and when they are able to continue working productively without help. It is essential that students have time to explore problems. Giving help too soon can deprive them of the opportunity to make mathematical discoveries. Students need to know that a challenging problem will take some time and that perseverance is an important aspect of the problem-solving process and of doing mathematics.

Classroom Applications

As students share their solutions with classmates, teachers can help them probe various aspects of their strategies. Explanations that are simply procedural descriptions or summaries should give way to mathematical arguments. Ms. Abreu has posed the following problem to her fifth-grade class:

I invited 8 people to a party (including me), and I had 12 brownies. How much did each person get if everyone got a fair share? Later my mother got home with 9 more brownies. We can always eat more brownies, so we shared these out equally too. This time, how much brownie did each person get? How much brownie did each person eat altogether?

In this vignette (adapted from Kazemi, 1998), we listen in as she observes her students at work.

Ms. Abreu stops at the table where Fabiola and Marissa are working and asks them to explain how they divided the nine extra brownies among eight people. Marissa replies, "The first four we cut them in half." Ms. Abreu says, "Okay, could you explain why you did it in half?" Marissa says, "Because when you put it in half, it becomes four (she hesitates), eight halves."

Figure 6.3

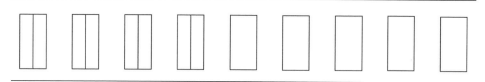

Ms. Abreu asks, "Eight halves? What does that mean if there are eight halves?" Marissa replies, "Then each person gets a half." Ms. Abreu says, "Okay, then each person gets a half."

Marissa continues, "Then there were five brownies left. We put them in eighths."

Figure 6.4

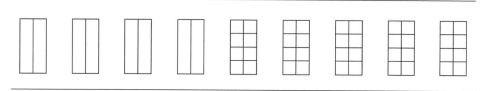

Ms. Abreu asks, "Okay, so you divided them into eighths. Could you tell me why you chose eighths?" Marissa replies, "It's easiest. Because then everyone will get (she hesitates), each person will get a half and (she speaks to Fabiola) how many eighths?" Fabiola quietly replies, "Five-eighths." Ms. Abreu replies, "I didn't know why you did it in eighths. That's the reason. I just wanted to know why you chose eighths." Fabiola replies, "We did eighths because then if we did eighths, each person would get each eighth, I mean one-eighth out of each brownie." Ms. Abreu says, "One-eighth. Okay. So how much, then, did they get if they got their fair share?" Marissa and Fabiola say together, "They got a half and five-eighths." Ms. Abreu asks, "Can you show me how much one person gets?" Fabiola thinks for a moment and draws.

Figure 6.5

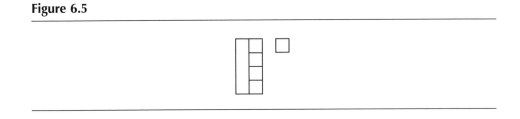

"One and one-eighth," she says.

During the discussion, Ms. Abreu pressed Marissa and Fabiola to give reasons for their decisions and actions: What does it mean if there are eight halves? Could you tell me why you chose eighths? Can you show me what you mean by that? She was not satisfied with a simple summary of the steps but instead expected the students to give verbal justifications all along the way and to connect those justifications with both numbers and representations.

Precautions and Possible Pitfalls

In any assessment of problem solving, teachers must look beyond the answer to the reasoning behind the solution. This requires that teachers pose appropriate and productive problems, listen carefully to student responses, and follow up with questions designed to help students communicate what they think and can do. Teachers also need to understand how students learn particular mathematical concepts and need to be aware of common misconceptions and strategies useful in addressing such misconceptions. As teachers become more familiar with their students—through analysis of written or oral work, explanations, or drawings—appropriate instructional decisions can be made (NCTM, 1995).

Sources

Kazemi, E. (1998). Discourse that promotes conceptual understanding. *Teaching Children Mathematics, 4,* 410–414.

NCTM. (1995). *Assessment standards for school mathematics.* Reston, VA: NCTM.

NCTM. (2000). *Principles and standards for school mathematics.* Reston, VA: NCTM.

Schoenfeld, A. H. (1992). Learning to think mathematically: Problem solving, metacognition, and sense making in mathematics. In D. Grouws (Ed.), *Handbook for research on mathematics teaching and learning* (pp. 334–370). New York: Macmillan.

7

Reasoning and Proof

Grades PreK–2

Young students are just forming their store of mathematical knowledge, but even the youngest can reason from their own experiences (Bransford, Brown, & Cocking, 1999). Although young children are working from a small knowledge base, their logical reasoning begins before school and is continually modified by their experiences. Teachers should maintain an environment that respects, nurtures, and encourages students so that they do not give up their belief that the world, including mathematics, is supposed to make sense.

Although they have yet to develop all the tools used in mathematical reasoning, young students have their own ways of finding mathematical results and convincing themselves that they are true. Two important elements of reasoning for students in the early grades are pattern-recognition and classification skills. They use a combination of ways of justifying their answers—perception, empirical evidence, and short chains of deductive reasoning grounded in previously accepted facts. They make conjectures and reach conclusions that are logical and defensible from their perspective. Even when they are struggling, their responses reveal the sense they are making of mathematical situations.

Young students naturally generalize from examples (Carpenter & Levi, 1999), so teachers should guide them to use examples and counterexamples to test whether their generalizations are appropriate. By the end of second grade, students should be using this method for testing their conjectures and those of others.

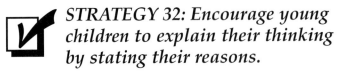

STRATEGY 32: *Encourage young children to explain their thinking by stating their reasons.*

NCTM Standard

What should reasoning and proof look like in Grades PreK through 2?

What Research and the NCTM Standards Say (NCTM, 2000)

The ability to reason systematically and carefully develops when students are encouraged to make conjectures, are given time to search for evidence to prove or disprove them, and are expected to explain and justify their ideas (Cobb et al., 1997). In the beginning, perception may be the predominant method of determining truth: nine markers spread far apart may be seen as "more" than eleven markers placed close together. Later, as students develop their mathematical tools, they should use empirical approaches such as matching the collections, which leads to the use of more abstract methods such as counting to compare the collections. Maturity, experiences, and increased mathematical knowledge together promote the development of reasoning throughout the early years.

Classroom Applications

Being able to explain one's thinking by stating reasons is an important skill for formal reasoning that begins at this level. Students must explain their chains of reasoning in order to see them clearly and use them more effectively. At the same time, teachers should model the mathematical language that students have not yet connected with their ideas. Ms. Austin-Page has been using unit blocks to help her kindergartners extend and develop their sense of space. In this vignette (adapted from Andrews, 1999), we listen as Ms. Austin-Page asks the class what they had learned today.

Jack waves his hand frantically saying, "I can prove that a triangle equals a square." Ms. Austin-Page asks Jack to tell the class more about his discovery, and Jack goes to the block corner and returns with two half-unit (square) blocks, two half-unit (triangle) blocks, and one unit (rectangle) block.

Figure 7.1

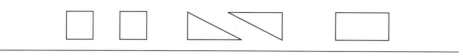

"See," he says proudly. "If these two (he holds up the square half-units) are the same as this one (he holds up the rectangular unit)

Figure 7.2

and these two (he now holds up the triangular half-units) are the same as this one (he holds up the rectangular unit again),

Figure 7.3

then this square has to be the same as this triangle (he holds up the square half-unit and the triangle half-unit)!"

Figure 7.4

Even though Jack's wording—that shapes were "equal"—was not correct, he was demonstrating powerful reasoning as he used the blocks to explain his idea. In situations such as this, Ms. Austin-Page might model the appropriate mathematics language by pointing to the faces of the two smaller blocks and responding, "You discovered that the area of this square equals the area of this triangle because each of them is half the area of the same larger rectangle?"

Precautions and Possible Pitfalls

 Young children often have difficulty solving problems if they begin working on a problem as soon as they or the teacher has finished reading the problem. Instead, children, after reading the problem, should be given opportunities to discuss and explore the problem and then encouraged to develop, as experts do, a problem-solving plan. Young children should also to be provided with time to practice their solution attempts (Posamentier, Hartman, & Kaiser, 1998). Giving help too soon can deprive children of the opportunity to make mathematical discoveries. Children need to know that a challenging problem will take some time and that perseverance is an important part of the reasoning process (NCTM, 2000).

Sources

Andrews, A. G. (1999). Solving geometric problems by using unit blocks. *Teaching Children Mathematics, 6*, 318–323.

Bransford, J. D., Brown, A. L., & Cocking, R. R. (1999). *How people learn: Brain, mind, experience, and school.* Washington, DC: National Academy Press.

Carpenter, T. P., & Levi, L. (1999). *Developing conceptions of algebraic reasoning in the primary grades.* Paper presented at the annual meeting of the American Educational Research Association, Montreal, April 1999.

Cobb, P., Boufi, A., McClain, K., & Whitenack, J. (1997). Reflective discourse and collective reflection. *Journal for Research in Mathematics Education, 28*, 258–277.

NCTM. (2000). *Principles and standards for school mathematics.* Reston, VA: NCTM.

Posamentier, A. S., Hartman, H. J., & Kaiser, C. (1998). *Tips for the mathematics teacher: Research-based strategies to help students learn.* Thousand Oaks, CA: Corwin Press.

STRATEGY 33: Ask questions that encourage young children to make conjectures and to justify their thinking.

NCTM Standard

What should be the teacher's role in developing reasoning and proof in Grades PreK through 2?

What Research and the NCTM Standards Say (NCTM, 2000)

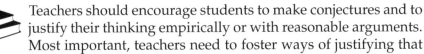

Teachers should encourage students to make conjectures and to justify their thinking empirically or with reasonable arguments. Most important, teachers need to foster ways of justifying that are within the reach of students, that do not rely on authority, and that gradually incorporate mathematical properties and relationships as the basis for the argument (McClain & Cobb, 1999). When students make a discovery or determine a fact, rather than telling them whether it holds for all numbers or if it is correct, the teacher should help the students make that determination by themselves. Teachers should ask questions such as "How do you know it is true?" and should model ways that students might use to verify or disprove their conjectures. In this way, students gradually develop the abilities to determine whether an assertion is true, a generalization is valid, or an answer is correct and to do it on their own instead of depending on the authority of the teacher or the text.

Classroom Applications

Ms. Foster has done more number work with her kindergarten class this year, and she is pleased with what her students are doing. Now, near the end of the year, her class has been investigating patterns in the number of various body parts—for example, how many noses or eyes there are among the students in the class. Earlier in the week, each student has made a nose out of clay. In this vignette (adapted from NCTM, 1991, Vignette 2.1), we listen as Ms. Foster asks the class, "And how many noses did we make?"

Becky points to her nostrils and says, "Two of these." Ms. Foster smiles and says, "But how many actual noses?" Ann speaks up, "Twenty-nine." Ms. Foster replies, "Why? Why were there twenty-nine noses?" Adam raises his hand and says, "Because every kid in the class made one clay nose and that is the same number as kids in the class."

Ms. Foster (pointing to her nostrils) says, "Now, Becky just said— remember what these are called?" The students chant, "Nostrils!" Ms. Foster continues, "So were there twenty-nine nostrils?" Pat raises her hand and says, "No, there were more." Gwen shouts, "Fifty-eight! We had fifty-eight nostrils!" Ms. Foster says, "Why fifty-eight?" Gwen replies, "I counted." Felice speaks quietly. "If we had thirty kids, we would be sixty. So it is fifty-nine 'cause it should be one less." "Felice," Ms. Foster says, "can you say that again? I don't think Anthony could hear you." Felice says, "It's fifty-nine because we don't have thirty kids, we have twenty-nine, so it is one less than sixty."

Ms. Foster looks around the class and asks, "What does anyone else think?" Adam raises his hand and says, "I think it is fifty-eight. Each kid has two nostrils. So if sixty would be for thirty kids, then it has to be two less: fifty-eight." Lawrence speaks up, "But Felice says thirty kids makes sixty . . ." Felice interrupts, "No! That makes sense. Fifty-eight." Ms. Foster again looks around the class and says, "What do you think?" Several children chorus, "Fifty-eight." Ms. Foster says, "So it's fifty-eight because thirty kids would have sixty nostrils and we have to take away two for one less kid. Gwen said she counted. Let's count and see."

Ms. Foster consistently encourages her students to explain and justify their answers. "Why?" is a standard response, asked about apparently correct as well as apparently incorrect answers. Ms. Foster also solicits other students' reactions instead of showing them the right answer. Her tone of voice and her questions show the students that she expects and values their thinking.

To maintain student interest in a classmate's response, Ms. Foster also avoids repeating a student response if it was inaudible to others (Posamentier, Hartman, & Kaiser, 1998). For example, she requests that Felice, who speaks quietly, repeat her response so that it is audible to her classmates.

Precautions and Possible Pitfalls

There are certain questions that a teacher might wish to avoid—for example, consider the difference between "How many noses did we make?" and "Did we make twenty-nine noses?" In the former case, the students themselves are asked to determine the answer; in the latter case, the teacher provides the answer and asks for confirmation. There are also questioning techniques that merit consideration. In the early elementary grades, there is a fine line between respectfully modeling appropriate mathematical language—for example, "Joshua says that the triangle and the square are equal. Do you mean they have equal areas, Joshua?"—and merely repeating, more precisely, what a student has said—"So, the triangle and the square have equal areas. Okay?"

Sources

McClain, K., & Cobb, P. (1999). Supporting students' ways of reasoning about patterns and partitions. In J. V. Copley (Ed.), *Mathematics in the early years* (pp. 162–168). Reston, VA: NCTM.

NCTM. (1991). *Professional standards for teaching mathematics.* Reston, VA: NCTM.

NCTM. (2000). *Principles and standards for school mathematics.* Reston, VA: NCTM.

Posamentier, A. S., Hartman, H. J., & Kaiser, C. (1998). *Tips for the mathematics teacher: Research-based strategies to help students learn.* Thousand Oaks, CA: Corwin Press.

Grades 3–5

During Grades 3–5, students should be involved in an important transition in their mathematical reasoning. Many students begin this grade band believing that something is true because it has occurred before, because they have seen several examples of it, or because their experience to date seems to confirm it. During these grades, formulating conjectures and assessing them on the basis of evidence should become the norm. Students should learn that several examples are not sufficient to establish the truth of a conjecture and that counterexamples can be used to disprove a conjecture. They should learn that by considering a range of examples, they can reason about the general properties and relationships they find.

Mathematical reasoning develops in classrooms where students are encouraged to put forth their own ideas for examination. Teachers and students should be open to questions, reactions, and elaborations from others in the classroom. Students need to explain and justify their thinking and learn how to detect fallacies and critique others' thinking. They need to have ample opportunity to apply their reasoning skills and justify their thinking in mathematics discussions. They will need time, many varied and rich experiences, and guidance to develop the ability to construct valid arguments and to evaluate the arguments of others. There is clear evidence that in classrooms where reasoning is emphasized, students do engage in reasoning and, in the process, learn what constitutes acceptable mathematical explanation (Lampert, 1990; Yackel & Cobb 1994, 1996).

Much of the work in these grades should be focused on reasoning about mathematical relationships, such as the structure of a pattern, the similarities and differences between two classes of shapes, or the overall shape of the data represented on a line plot. Students should move from considering individual mathematical objects—this triangle, this number, this data point—to thinking about classes of objects—all triangles, all numbers that are multiples of 4, a whole set of data. Further, they should be developing descriptions and mathematical statements about relationships between these classes of objects, so that they can begin to understand the role of definition in mathematics (NCTM, 2000).

STRATEGY 34: Encourage students to reason about the relationships that apply to the numbers, operations, or shapes that they are studying.

NCTM Standard

 What should reasoning and proof look like in Grades 3 through 5?

What Research and the NCTM Standards Say (NCTM, 2000)

In Grades 3–5, students should reason about the relationships that apply to the numbers, shapes, or operations they are studying. They need to define the relationship, analyze why it is true, and determine to what group of mathematical objects (numbers, shapes, and operations) it can be applied. Students should frequently make conjectures about mathematical relationships, investigate those conjectures, and make mathematical arguments that are based on their work (Yackel & Hanna, 2003). They need to know that posing conjectures and trying to justify them is an expected part of students' mathematical activity. Justification will have a range of meanings for students in Grades 3–5, but as they progress through these grades and have more experiences with making mathematical arguments, they should increasingly base their arguments on an analysis of properties, structures, and relationships.

Classroom Applications

Through comparing solutions and questioning one another's reasoning, students can begin to learn to describe relationships that hold across many instances and to develop and defend arguments about why those relationships can be generalized and to what cases they apply (Maher & Martino, 1996). In this vignette (adapted from NCTM, 2000, p. 189), we listen in as Ms. Taylor's third-grade class is discussing how to compute 4 × 8.

Matt explains, "I thought of two times eight, that's sixteen, then you just double it." Ms. Taylor asks several students to restate the idea and then asks the class, "Do you think Matt's way of multiplying by four—by doubling, then doubling again—works with problems other than four times eight?" The response from students is quite mixed, and Ms. Taylor asks them to try some problems like this one themselves before gathering again to discuss Matt's method.

After students had worked on several problems and had discussed with a partner why "doubling, then doubling again" was a strategy for multiplying by 4, Ms. Taylor brought the class together for further discussion. Student responses to whether Matt's strategy would always work showed a wide range of thinking:

Carol: Because if you have two times eight and four times eight, you're doubling the answer. It works every time.

Malia: It has to be doubled because you're doing the same thing over again. It's like you did two times eight is sixteen and then you did two times eight is sixteen again, so it has to be thirty-two.

Steven: What you're doing is counting by eights, so you're counting ahead, you're skipping some of the eights. You're doing another two of them, so it's like doubling them up.

Matt: I tried to see if it would work with triples, so I did two times eight and six times eight, and it worked. You times it by three and the answer is tripled.

These students' explanations are tied to the specific example, but there is evidence that some students are constructing arguments that may lead to more general conclusions. Carol is satisfied that "it works every time" but does not have an argument that is based on the structure of multiplication. Malia refers to breaking up one of the factors in the problem into two parts [$4 \times 8 = (2 + 2) \times 8$], multiplying the other number by both parts ($4 \times 8 = 2 \times 8 + 2 \times 8$), and then adding the results ($4 \times 8 = 16 + 16$)—that is, the distributive property of multiplication over addition. Steven's explanation is based on modeling multiplication as skip-counting, and Matt takes his original idea further by testing whether multiplying by six is the same as multiplying by two, then by three [$(6 \times 8 = 3 \times (2 \times 8)$)]—that is, the associative property of multiplication. Although none of these third graders' arguments is stated in a way that is complete or general, they are beginning to see what it means to develop and test conjectures about mathematical relationships.

Precautions and Possible Pitfalls

Sometimes students' conjectures about mathematical properties and relationships will turn out to be wrong. Part of mathematical reasoning is examining and trying to understand why something that looks and seems as if it might be true is not and to begin to use counterexamples in this context. Coming up with ideas that turn out not to be true is part of the endeavor. These "wrong" ideas often are opportunities for important mathematical discussions and discoveries. For example, a student might propose that if both the numerator and denominator of a fraction are larger than the numerator and denominator, respectively, of another fraction, then the first fraction must be larger. This rule works in comparing 3/4 with 1/2 or 6/4 with 2/3. However, when thinking about this conjecture more carefully, students will find counterexamples—for example, 3/4 is not larger than 2/2 and 2/6 is smaller than 1/2.

Sources

Lampert, M. (1990). When the problem is not the question and the solution is not the answer: Mathematical knowing and teaching. *American Educational Research Journal, 27,* 29–63.

Maher, C. A., & Martino, A. M. (1996). The development of the idea of mathematical proof: A five-year case study. *Journal for Research in Mathematics Education, 27,* 194–214.

NCTM. (2000). *Principles and standards for school mathematics.* Reston, VA: NCTM.

Yackel, E., & Cobb, P. (1994). *The development of young children's understanding of mathematical argumentation.* Paper presented at the annual meeting of the American Educational Research Association, New Orleans.

Yackel, E., & Cobb, P. (1996). Sociomathematical norms, argumentation, and autonomy in mathematics. *Journal for Research in Mathematics Education, 27,* 458–477.

Yackel, E., & Hanna, G. (2003). Reasoning and proof. In J. Kilpatrick, W. G. Martin, & D. Shifter (Eds.), *A research companion to* Principles and standards for school mathematics. Reston, VA: NCTM.

STRATEGY 35: *Focus on general mathematical structures and relationships.*

NCTM Standard

What should be the teacher's role in developing reasoning and proof in Grades 3 through 5?

What Research and the NCTM Standards Say (NCTM, 2000)

In order that mathematical experiences supporting reasoning and proof happen frequently, the teacher needs to establish the expectation that the class as a mathematical community is publicly developing, testing, and applying conjectures about mathematical relationships (Ball & Bass, 2003). This requires that teachers look for opportunities to go beyond finding the solution to an individual problem and focus on more general mathematical structures and relationships. Teachers will also have to make decisions about which conjectures are mathematically significant for students to pursue. To do this, the teacher needs to take into account the skills, needs, and understandings of the students and the mathematical goals for the class.

Classroom Applications

Part of the teacher's role in making reasoning central is to make all students responsible both for articulating their own reasoning and for working hard to understand the reasoning of others. Mr. Salazar's fourth graders have

been working on ordering fractions, and he has asked his students, working in pairs, to identify fractions that are more than 1/2 and less than 1. In this vignette (adapted from NCTM, 2000, pp. 191–192), we listen as his students discuss their conclusions.

Mr. Salazar asks the class how they were choosing their fractions. Derrick raises his hand. "We were talking about how you could get it, and if you make the top number, the numerator, higher than a half of the denominator, but you don't make it the same as the denominator like five-fifths 'cause then it will be a whole." Mr. Salazar replies, "It sounds like you have a conjecture. Can someone else explain it?" Jack speaks up, "Like if you have three-fourths, half of four is two, so you want the number higher than two but not four."

"How about five-elevenths? Does Derrick's conjecture work for five-elevenths?" Mr. Salazar asks. Jael replies, "Well, half of eleven is five and a half, so five-elevenths is less than one-half." "How about two-thirds?" Mr. Salazar asks. Roberto raises his hand. "Half of three is one and a half. So two-thirds works." Mr. Salazar replies, "Okay. But Derrick said something about not being able to make the numerator the same as the denominator." Masa waves her hand. "I know. The numerator has to be smaller than the denominator and two is smaller than three."

By routinely questioning students in this way, Mr. Salazar is establishing the expectation that students listen carefully to one another's ideas and attempt to understand them and is focusing their attention on general mathematical structures and relationships. Mr. Salazar might also look for opportunities for his students to revise, expand, and update generalizations they have made as they develop new mathematical skills and insights.

Precautions and Possible Pitfalls

 Developing a child's ability to reason systematically and carefully requires more than encouragement, and merely posing challenging problems or asking children to explain their thinking is insufficient. Teaching such reasoning requires both pedagogy and design just as any other aspect of mathematics. Two suggestions (Ball & Bass, 2003) are to

- design mathematical tasks that create a demand for mathematical reasoning.
- make students' mathematical work public and help make such work comprehensible so that the work itself can become the focus for careful and audible articulation of mathematical ideas and for attentive listening.

Sources

Ball, D. L., & Bass, H. (2003). Making mathematics reasonable in school. In J. Kilpatrick, W. G. Martin, & D. Shifter (Eds.), *A research companion to Principles and standards for school mathematics.* Reston, VA: NCTM.

NCTM. (2000). *Principles and standards for school mathematics.* Reston, VA: NCTM.

8

Communication

Grades PreK–2

Language, whether used to express ideas or to receive them, is a very powerful tool and should be used to foster the learning of mathematics. Communicating about mathematical ideas is a way for students to articulate, clarify, organize, and consolidate their thinking. Students, like adults, exchange thoughts and ideas in many ways—orally, with gestures, and with pictures, objects, and symbols. By listening carefully to others, students can become aware of alternative perspectives and strategies. By writing and talking with others, they learn to use more precise mathematical language and, gradually, conventional symbols to express their mathematical ideas. Communication makes mathematical thinking observable and therefore facilitates further development of that thought. It encourages students to reflect on their own knowledge and their own ways of solving problems. Throughout the early years, students should have daily opportunities to talk and write about mathematics. They should become increasingly effective in communicating what they understand through their own notation and language as well as in conventional ways (NCTM, 2000).

STRATEGY 36: *Encourage young children's verbal and written communication of mathematics concepts and ideas.*

NCTM Standard

What should communication look like in Grades PreK through 2?

What Research and the NCTM Standards Say (NCTM, 2000)

Children begin to communicate mathematically very early in their lives. They want more milk, a different toy, or three books. The communication abilities of most children have developed tremendously before they enter kindergarten. This growth is determined to a large extent by the children's maturity, how language is modeled for them, and their opportunities and experiences. Verbal interaction with families and caregivers is a primary means for promoting the development of early mathematical vocabulary.

Language is as important to learning mathematics as it is to learning to read. As students enter school, their opportunities to communicate are expanded by new learning resources, enriched uses of language, and experiences with classmates and teachers. Students' developing communication skills can be used to organize and consolidate their mathematical thinking. Teachers should help students learn how to talk about mathematics, to explain their answers, and to describe their strategies. Teachers can encourage students to reflect on class conversations and to "talk about talking about mathematics" (Cobb, Wood, & Yackel, 1994).

Classroom Applications

Young students' abilities to talk and listen are usually more advanced than their abilities to read and write, especially in the early years of this grade band. Therefore, teachers must be diligent in providing experiences that allow varied forms of communication as a natural component of mathematics class. Ms. Daley has repeatedly read and her kindergarten class has actively dramatized the movement patterns in A Week of Raccoons, *by Gloria Whelan (1990). In this vignette (adapted from Andrews, 1996), we listen in as Ms. Daley asks her kindergartners to recall and illustrate on paper the detailed journey Mr. Twerkle—the hero of the story—takes as he resettles a family of raccoons from his farm, past a tumble-down log cabin, around an old apple tree, and over the bridge to the "piney woods."*

The students work individually and then, in groups, they use their drawings to make a large map of Mr. Twerkle's journey. They decide how to divide the task of map making and where to place points of interest. When the maps are completed, they are hung along the walls of the hallway so that the kindergartners can study them and retrace Mr. Twerkle's route with their fingers. Often students, in referring to the maps, reenact the journey with their hands or entire bodies. Some of the conversation that such observations generate are written on speech bubbles by Ms. Daley and placed near the work. Comments include: "I think the part where Mr. Twerkle goes over the bridge should be more near the log house than the apple tree"; "Next time, we should start our map closer to the top. See. We ran off the page here"; and "I like the way you made the fish jumping out of the water running under the bridge. It is jumping really high." Within this activity, Ms. Daley has provided opportunities for students to communicate their observations and ideas about the geometric world in which they live. Such terms as *really high, more near,* and *closer to the top* are precursors to complex mathematical concepts that will be introduced in later grades.

Precautions and Possible Pitfalls

On the basis of written language, teachers often underestimate young children's mathematical capabilities. Young children's abilities to talk and listen are usually more advanced than their abilities to read and write, especially in the preK years. Thus, young children can both talk about their mathematics experiences and dictate their mathematical ideas to others. Further, although most four- and five-year-olds will be unable to record their mathematical thoughts and ideas in written form, they can use visual representations to record and, hence, communicate their investigations of and experiences with space (Andrews, 1996).

Sources

Andrews, A. G. (1996). Developing spatial sense—a moving experience! *Teaching Children Mathematics, 2,* 290–293.

Cobb, P., Wood, T., & Yackel, E. (1994). Discourse, mathematical thinking, and classroom practice. In E. A. Forman, N. Minick, & C. A. Stone (Eds.), *Contexts for learning: Sociocultural dynamics in children's development* (pp. 91–119). New York: Oxford University Press.

NCTM. (2000). *Principles and standards for school mathematics.* Reston, VA: NCTM.

Whelan, G. (1990). *A week of raccoons.* New York: Greenwillow Press.

STRATEGY 37: *Expect young children to explain their thinking and give them opportunities to talk with and listen to their peers.*

NCTM Standard

What should be the teacher's role in developing communication in Grades PreK through 2?

What Research and the NCTM Standards Say (NCTM, 2000)

Teachers can create and structure mathematically rich environments for students in a number of ways. They should present problems that challenge students mathematically, but they should also let students know they believe that the students can solve them. They should expect students to explain their thinking and should give students many opportunities to talk with, and listen to, their peers (Lampert & Cobb, 2003). Teachers should recognize that learning to analyze and reflect on what is said by others is essential in developing an understanding of both content and process. When it is difficult for young learners to follow the reasoning of a classmate, teachers can help by guiding students to rephrase their reasoning in words that are easier for themselves and others to understand. Teachers should model appropriate conventional vocabulary and help students build such vocabulary on the basis of shared knowledge and processes.

Classroom Applications

Building a community of learners, where students exchange mathematical ideas not only with the teacher but also with one another, should be a goal in every classroom. In this vignette (adapted from NCTM, 2000, p. 131), we listen in as Ms. Jensen poses the following question to her first-grade class:

How many books do I need to return to the library if I have three nonfiction and four fiction books?

Maury, who seldom shares his answers with the class, speaks out, "Seven." In the past, if Ms. Jensen asked him how he figured out a problem, Maury just shrugged his shoulders. This time, however, Ms. Jensen decides to involve another student and asks Jessica, "How do you think Maury figured it out?" Jessica holds up three fingers as she answers, "I think he did it this way. I know there are three, so I just put up four more fingers and then count them all." This prompts Maury to respond, "I did it a different way. I just knew that three and three make six and then I counted one more."

Ms. Jensen, rather than confirming Maury's answer, sets the stage for two of her students to explain their methods and for the classroom community to hear and discuss these and other ways of thinking about the same problem. Opportunities such as this encourage students to listen to one another and to reflect on, analyze, and talk about what they see and hear.

Precautions and Possible Pitfalls

Teachers need to be aware that the patterns of communication between students and adults in the school may not necessarily match the patterns of communication in students' homes. For example, patterns of questioning can be very different. In some cultures, adults generally do not ask questions when the answer is known; they ask questions primarily to seek information that they do not have (Bransford, Brown, & Cocking, 1999). In school, however, teachers frequently ask questions to which the answer is known. Students who are not accustomed to such questions can be bewildered, since it is obvious that the teacher already knows the answers. Similarly, in some cultures, people routinely interrupt one another in conversations, whereas in others, interruptions are considered extremely rude. Thus, students from the first group may unduly dominate class discussions (NCTM, 2000).

Teachers need to be aware of the cultural patterns in their students' home communities in order to provide equitable opportunities for them to communicate their mathematical thinking. Activities can be designed that encourage individual and group inquiry. Teachers can invest in questions to which they do not have firm answers—for example, "How do you know?" or "Can somebody explain how Maury got seven?" Conversation classroom norms can be instituted that provide space for excited interruptions as well as space for respectful listening and reflection. All children deserve appropriate opportunities to communicate their mathematical thinking.

Sources

Bransford, J. D., Brown, A. L., & Cocking, R. R. (Eds.). (1999). *How people learn: Brain, mind, experience, and school.* Washington, DC: National Academy Press.
Lampert, M., & Cobb, P. (2003). Communication and language. In J. Kilpatrick, W. G. Martin, & D. Shifter (Eds.), *A research companion to* Principles and standards for school mathematics. Reston, VA: NCTM.
NCTM. (2000). *Principles and standards for school mathematics.* Reston, VA: NCTM.

Grades 3–5

The ability to read, write, listen, think, and communicate about problems will develop and deepen students' understanding of mathematics. In Grades 3–5, students should use communication as a tool for understanding and generating solution strategies. Their writing should be more coherent than in earlier grades, and their increasing mathematical vocabulary can be used along with everyday language to explain concepts. Depending on the purpose for writing, such as taking notes or writing to explain an answer, students' descriptions of problem-solving strategies and reasoning should become more detailed and coherent (NCTM, 2000).

In Grades 3–5, students should become more adept at learning from and working with others. Their communication can consist not only of conversations between student and teacher or one student and another student but also of students listening to a number of peers and joining group discussions in order to clarify, question, and extend conjectures. In classroom discussions, students should become the audience for one another's comments. This involves speaking to one another in order to convince or question peers. The discourse should not be a goal in itself but rather should be focused on making sense of mathematical ideas and using them effectively in modeling and solving problems. The value of mathematical discussions is determined by whether students are learning as they participate in them (Lampert & Cobb, 2003).

STRATEGY 38: Encourage students to share their thinking, to ask questions, and to justify their ideas.

NCTM Standard

 What should communication look like in Grades 3 through 5?

What Research and the NCTM Standards Say (NCTM, 2000)

In a Grades 3–5 classroom, communication should include sharing thinking, asking questions, and explaining and justifying ideas. It should be well integrated into the classroom environment. Students should be encouraged to express and write about their mathematical conjectures, questions, and solutions. The use of models and pictures can provide further opportunities for understanding and conversation. Having a concrete referent helps students develop understandings that are clearer and more easily shared (Hiebert et al., 1997).

Classroom Applications

Ms. Stowe's fifth-grade class has been working with decimals. Although her class has discussed how to represent decimals, they have not discussed how to add them. Ms. Stowe wants to help her fifth graders think about and develop skills for adding decimals. She also wants to help her students further develop their communication skills, to talk productively with their peers about solving the problem, and to share their results and thinking with the class. With these goals in mind, she has designed the following problem:

> Pretend you are a jeweler. Sometimes people come in to get rings resized. When you cut down a ring to make it smaller, you keep the small portion of gold in exchange for the work you have done. Recently you have collected these amounts:
>
> 1.14 grams, .089 grams, and .3 grams
>
> Now you have a repair job to do for which you need some gold. You are wondering if you have enough. Work together with your group to figure out how much gold you have collected. Be prepared to show the class your solution.

In this vignette (adapted from Schifter, Bastable, & Russell, 1999, Case 28), we listen in as Ms. Stowe circulates among the working students.

She stops to listen to Jeanine, Paul, and Steve. Jeanine looks up and says, "We could line the numbers up on the right like you do with other numbers." Paul adds, "Maybe we should line up the decimals, but I don't know why we would do that." Ms. Stowe replies, "I think you're suggesting that you might line this problem up differently from the way you line up whole-number addition. Is that right?" Paul nods. Ms. Stowe continues, "Why do you line whole numbers up the way you do? What's the reason for it?" Paul looks puzzled. "I don't know. It's just the way you do it. That's how we learned to do it." Steve says quietly, "I think it would help if we drew a picture, like of the base-ten blocks."

After the groups finished their work, the class as a whole had a discussion. Eric reported that the students in his group represented the problem as the following:

$$
\begin{array}{r}
\overset{1}{} \\
.3 \quad \text{gram} \\
1.14 \quad \text{gram} \\
+ \ .089 \ \text{gram} \\
\hline
1.529 \ \text{gram}
\end{array}
$$

Paul immediately asked why they had decided to line up the numbers that way, and Eric responded that the group thought, just as with whole-number addition, they needed to line up the tenths with the tenths and the hundredths with the hundredths to "make it come out right."

Because discussion of thinking was a regular occurrence in Ms. Stowe's classroom, students were comfortable describing their thinking, even if their ideas were different from the ideas of their peers. Besides focusing on their own thinking, students also attempted to understand the thinking of others and in some cases to relate it to their own. Paul, who earlier had been unable to articulate why he lined up whole numbers in a particular way when he added, questioned Eric about why his group had lined up the numbers the way they did. Paul was taking responsibility for his learning by asking questions about a concept that wasn't quite clear to him.

Precautions and Possible Pitfalls

Discussions such as that taking place among Ms. Stowe's students do not, in general, just happen. Teachers shape the discourse of their classrooms through the signals they send, consciously or unconsciously, about how knowledge is to be valued, constructed, and exchanged (Ball, 1991). Ms. Stowe must take a central role in structuring the classroom culture and in orchestrating oral and written discourse in ways that contribute to students' understanding of mathematics. This includes provoking students' reasoning about mathematics; expecting students to talk, model, and explain themselves; modeling respect for students' thinking; and conveying the assumption that what students communicate makes sense (NCTM, 1991).

Sources

Ball, D. L. (1991). What's all this talk about "discourse"? *Arithmetic Teacher, 39,* 44–48.

Hiebert, J., Carpenter, T. P., Fennema, E., Fuson, K. C., Wearne, D., Murray, H., Olivier, A., & Human, P. (1997). *Making sense: Teaching and learning mathematics with understanding.* Portsmouth, NH: Heinemann.

Lampert, M., & Cobb, P. (2003). Communication and language. In J. Kilpatrick, W. G. Martin, & D. Shifter (Eds.), *A research companion to* Principles and standards for school mathematics. Reston, VA: NCTM.

NCTM. (1991). *Professional standards for teaching mathematics.* Reston, VA: NCTM.

NCTM. (2000). *Principles and standards for school mathematics.* Reston, VA: NCTM.

Schifter, D., Bastable, B., & Russell, S. J. (1999). *Building a system of tens casebook. Developing mathematical ideas: Number and operations, Part 1.* Parsippany, NJ: Dale Seymour Publications.

STRATEGY 39: *Provide models for student dialogue about mathematics.*

NCTM Standard

What should be the teacher's role in developing communication in Grades 3 through 5?

What Research and the NCTM Standards Say (NCTM, 2000)

With appropriate support and a classroom environment where communication about mathematics is expected, teachers can work to build the capacity of students to think, reason, solve complex problems, and communicate mathematically. This involves creating classroom environments in which intellectual risks and sense making are expected. Teachers must also routinely provide students with rich problems centered on the important mathematical ideas in the curriculum so that students are working with situations worthy of their conversation and thought. In daily lessons, teachers must make on-the-spot decisions about which points of the mathematical conversation to pick up on and which to let go, and when to let students struggle with an issue and when to give direction. Teachers must refine their listening, questioning, and paraphrasing techniques, both to direct the flow of mathematical learning and to provide models for student dialogue (Lampert & Cobb, 2003).

Classroom Applications

Periodically, teachers need to talk about "talking about mathematics" (Lampert & Cobb, 2003). For example, teachers might model questioning and explaining and then point out and explain those techniques to their students. Ms. Paulino and her third graders have been reviewing their addition facts. In order to challenge and extend her students' thinking, Ms. Paulino has posed the following problem to the class:

Write number sentences for 10.

In this vignette (adapted from Ball & Bass, 2003), we listen in as Ms. Paulino asks her class for their solutions.

Charles raises his hand and says, "Four plus six is ten." Several children nod their heads, and Annalisa says, "I got eight plus two." Ms. Paulino asks, "Can someone make a number sentence that equals ten, but has more than two numbers adding up to ten?" Derrick speaks up, "One plus one plus one plus one plus one. Plus five."

Ms. Paulino writes his answer on the board and turns to Robin. "Why does that equal ten?" she asks. Robin says, "Because one plus one plus one plus one plus one plus five equals ten." Ms. Paulino replies, "You're just sort of reading it. How could you prove it to somebody who wasn't sure?" Robin hesitates and says, "Because I counted it." Ms. Paulino nods and says, "What did you count? What did you find out?" Robin speaks slowly. "There's one and the next one is two and the next one is three, next one is four, next one is five, then five more, six, seven, eight, nine, ten." Ms. Paulino turns to the class and says, "Do you see the difference in Robin's second explanation? Did you see how she really showed us how it equals ten?" She turns to Robin and continues, "The first time you just read it. And the second time you explained it. That was really nice."

Here Ms. Paulino does more than praise Robin. She points to the mathematical explanation Robin has constructed and conveys expectations as to what it might mean to communicate mathematically. Discussion of various student responses, especially as mathematical concepts and problems become more complex, is an effective way to help students continue to improve their ability to communicate mathematics.

Precautions and Possible Pitfalls

In addition to providing assistance with students' oral mathematics explanations, teachers also need to provide students with assistance in writing about mathematics concepts. Teachers should expect students' writing to be correct, complete, coherent, and clear. Students will also need opportunities to check the clarity of their work with peers. When students initially have difficulty knowing what to write about in mathematics class, the teacher might ask them to use words, drawings, and symbols to explain a particular mathematical idea. For example, students in the upper elementary grades might write about how they know that 1/2 is greater than 2/5 and show at least three different ways to justify this conclusion.

Sources

Ball, D. L., & Bass, H. (2003). Making mathematics reasonable in school. In J. Kilpatrick, W. G. Martin, & D. Shifter (Eds.), *A research companion to* Principles and standards for school mathematics. Reston, VA: NCTM.

Lampert, M., & Cobb, P. (2003). Communication and language. In J. Kilpatrick, W. G. Martin, & D. Shifter (Eds.), *A research companion to* Principles and standards for school mathematics. Reston, VA: NCTM.

NCTM. (2000). *Principles and standards for school mathematics.* Reston, VA: NCTM.

9

Connections

Grades PreK–2

The most important connection for early mathematics development is between the intuitive, informal mathematics that students have learned through their own experiences and the mathematics they are learning in school. All other connections—between one mathematical concept and another, between different mathematics topics, between mathematics and other fields of knowledge, and between mathematics and everyday life—are supported by the link between the students' informal experiences and more formal mathematics. Students' abilities to experience mathematics as a meaningful endeavor that makes sense rest on these connections (NCTM, 2000).

 STRATEGY 40: Encourage young children to make connections among mathematical ideas, vocabulary, and representations.

NCTM Standard

 What should connections look like in Grades PreK through 2?

What Research and the NCTM Standards Say (NCTM, 2000)

Young children often connect new mathematical ideas with old ones by using concrete objects. When a preschool child holds up three fingers and asks an adult, "Am I this many years old?" he is trying to connect the word three with the number that represents his age through a set of concrete objects, his fingers. Teachers should encourage students to use their own strategies to make connections among mathematical ideas, the vocabulary associated with the ideas, and the ways the ideas are represented. For example, students frequently use objects and counting strategies as they develop their understanding of addition and subtraction and connect the two operations (Fuson, 2004).

Classroom Applications

Students can better understand relationships among the many aspects of mathematics if they engage in connected and purposeful activities. Ms. Minta's first graders have counted sets of objects many times and have had a number of experiences in estimating quantities of objects up to 35 or 40. Ms. Minta wants to see if her students can apply their mathematics knowledge to a more complex situation. In this vignette (adapted from Micklo, 1999), we listen in as Ms. Minta discusses estimation with her class.

Ms. Minta first emphasizes to her class that "Estimation is not a guess. To make a guess, you do not have to think about how many there are. Any number can be a guess. To make an estimate, you have to think." She then takes a handful of marbles from a container and begins to place them in a jar. She counts out loud, ". . . sixteen, seventeen, eighteen. I just placed eighteen marbles into this jar." Her class watches her intently as she picks up a second similar handful of marbles and places them in the jar without counting them. She then places a third and fourth handful in the jar without counting them. The jar cannot hold another complete handful, so Ms. Minta picks up a smaller amount and places that in the jar so that the jar is almost full.

Ms. Minta looks at her class and says, "Now, I want you to think and give me an estimate of about how many marbles are in the jar. Don't guess. Think about what I just did with the marbles and give me an estimate." Amma raises her hand and says, "I know, fifty-three!" Ms. Minta nods and says, "Okay. However, remember the other day when we were talking about *nice numbers*, those numbers that are easy to use? Would you like to give me your estimate again?" Amma replies, "Fifty!" Ms. Minta says, "Okay. Gabriel and then Brendaliz." Gabriel replies, "One hundred," and Brendaliz offers, "One thousand." This continues until several estimates, ranging from 20 to 1,000, have been written on the board. "Any more?"

Ms. Minta asks. "Then let's all look at the estimates and talk about what these might tell us about how many marbles are in the jar. Remember, I put eighteen marbles in the jar the first time and then put in about that many again, then again, then again. Then I added a small amount."

Kathleen raises her hand. "Well, if you put in eighteen marbles and then more handfuls, there would be more than twenty marbles." Miriam adds, "And there are not a thousand marbles. That would be a lot of marbles and the jar is too small. Eighteen is close to twenty, and twenty and twenty are forty, and forty and forty are eighty, and a few more maybe make ninety marbles." Ms. Minta says, "So you think there are about ninety marbles in the jar? Anyone with another idea?" Rick raises his hand. "Maybe there were more, maybe it is one hundred." Ms. Minta says, "So, some of you think the total could be close to ninety or one hundred. Estimates that are close to the total are called reasonable estimates. Based on your reasoning, we can say that ninety and one hundred are reasonable estimates."

By incorporating discussion and thinking into her lessons, Ms. Minta gives her students opportunities to connect the meaning of estimation to their previous understandings of numbers and addition. This allows the students to see that estimation is not the same as guessing; rather, it is a systematic method of thinking that can be used to solve real problems.

Precautions and Possible Pitfalls

Estimation can be taught in ways that are counterproductive; for example, children can be given several straightforward addition problems and then instructed to estimate before adding. The usual outcome in such a case is that a child carefully and skillfully adds and then rounds the exact answer to some appropriate number. This is not estimation. Estimation is a relatively quick and reasonable approximation to some measure or computation. Children should be provided with problem contexts that call for a range of reasonable answers rather than the exact answer. For example, given the expression

$$47 + 62$$

a first-grade teacher might ask: "about" how large the sum is; what is it "just about" or what is it "close to"; what numbers is it "between"; or what numbers is it "a little more (less) than" (Micklo, 1999).

Sources

Fuson, K. C. (2004). Pre-K to Grade 2 goals and standards: Achieving 21st-century mastery for all. *Engaging Young Children in Mathematics*. Mahwah, NJ: Lawrence Erlbaum Associates.

Micklo, S. J. (1999). Estimation: It's more than a guess. *Childhood Education, 75,* 142–145.

NCTM. (2000). *Principles and standards for school mathematics.* Reston, VA: NCTM.

STRATEGY 41: *Make links between routine school activities and mathematics.*

NCTM Standard

What should be the teacher's role in developing connections in Grades PreK through 2?

What Research and the NCTM Standards Say (NCTM, 2000)

In classrooms where connecting mathematical ideas is a focus, lessons are fluid and take many different formats. Teachers should ensure that links are made between routine school activities and mathematics by asking questions that emphasize the mathematical aspects of situations. They should plan tasks in new contexts that revisit topics previously taught, enabling students to forge new links between previously learned mathematical concepts and procedures and new applications, always with an eye on their mathematics goals. When teachers help students make explicit connections—mathematics to other mathematics and mathematics to other content areas—they are helping students learn to think mathematically (Lampert, 1989).

Classroom Applications

Mathematics is embedded in many activities that children do every day. In this vignette (adapted from Fosnot & Dolk, 2001, pp. 45–46), we listen in as Ms. Jackson and her class of four-year-olds discuss how many cartons of milk will be needed for snack. As a student makes a suggestion as to the number of cartons, Ms. Jackson, so as to see whether they will have enough, has them place one cardboard replica in each pocket in the attendance chart that contains a paper doll (indicating that child is in attendance). Seventeen pockets contain dolls, and the number 17 has been written next to the chart to indicate the day's attendance.

"So you wanted sixteen, Derelle? Okay, here are sixteen milks." Ms. Jackson gives Derelle 16 cardboard replicas, and, speaking to the class, says, "I wonder, do you think he will have enough for everyone today?"

Some students say "Yes," but others say "No." Derelle places a replica of a milk carton in each pocket in the attendance chart. "One," Robert speaks out. Ms. Jackson looks puzzled. "What did you say, Robert?" "One didn't get one," he explains. Ms. Jackson replies, "Yes, Natasha didn't get a milk. So is sixteen enough for everybody?" Derelle responds, "No, I need to give Natasha a milk."

Ms. Jackson doesn't give him another milk replica immediately. Instead, she asks the class, "How many more milks does he need?" All agree that one more is needed, so Ms. Jackson gives the replica to Derelle, and he places it in Natasha's attendance pocket. Ms. Jackson continues, "So you had sixteen, and that wasn't enough for everyone. We had to use one more. How many milks did we need, then?" Julius speaks up, "Seventeen." "You think seventeen, Julius. Well, let's see," Ms. Jackson replies. She gives Julius 17 replicas and he puts one in each of the attendance pockets. Ms. Jackson probes, "How did you know it was seventeen, Julius?" Julius replies, "'Cause seventeen is up there." He points to the attendance chart. "So if we see seventeen here, we know it's seventeen milks? Why do you think that is?" Ms. Jackson probes further, trying to engage other children as well. "'Cause it's seventeen children . . . ," Julius replies. Ms. Jackson asks, "Julius says there are seventeen children. So if there are seventeen children, then we need . . . ?" "Seventeen milks!" Julius confidently replies.

Note that Ms. Jackson has her students calculate and record the class attendance prior to the class discussion of how many milks are needed. This facilitates her students' noticing and connecting the *number* of milk cartons needed with the *number* of students present. Such activities as this can turn routine situations into situations that can be productively mathematized and systematically discussed.

Precautions and Possible Pitfalls

 Fosnot and Dolk (2001) point out that providing contexts that children can productively mathematize takes some forethought. Teachers need to provide situations that have, at a minimum, three components (Fosnot & Dolk, 2001):

- The situation lends itself to modeling; that is, the potential for modeling is "built in."
- The situation is one that children can make sense of; that is, it allows them "to realize what they are doing."
- The situation prompts children "to ask questions, notice patterns, wonder, ask why and what if."

Teachers should provide contexts that "simultaneously involve[s] children in problem solving and problem posing" (Fosnot & Dolk, 2001).

Sources

Fosnot, C. T., & Dolk, M. (2001). *Young mathematicians at work: Constructing number sense, addition, and subtraction.* Portsmouth, NH: Heinemann.

Lampert, M. (1989). Choosing and using mathematical tools in classroom discourse. In J. E. Brophy (Ed.), *Advances in research on teaching* (Vol. 1, pp. 223–264). Greenwich, CT: JAI Press.

NCTM. (2000). *Principles and standards for school mathematics.* Reston, VA: NCTM.

Grades 3–5

Students in Grades 3–5 study a considerable amount of new mathematical content, and their ability to understand and manage these new ideas will rest, in part, on how well the ideas are connected. Connecting mathematical ideas includes linking new ideas to related ideas considered previously. These connections help students see mathematics as a unified body of knowledge rather than as a set of complex and disjoint concepts, procedures, and processes (NCTM, 2000).

STRATEGY 42: Encourage students to see that mathematics is a web of closely connected ideas.

NCTM Standard

What should connections look like in Grades 3 through 5?

What Research and the NCTM Standards Say (NCTM, 2000)

Two big ideas that recur throughout the study of mathematics in Grades 3–5 are equivalence and multiplicative reasoning. Each should receive major emphasis at this level, in part because each is connected to so many topics studied in Grades 3–5. For example, students learn that a fraction has an equivalent decimal representation, that the area of a right triangle is equal to half of the area of a related rectangle, that 150 centimeters is the same as 1.5 meters, and that the likelihood of getting heads when flipping a coin is the same as the likelihood of rolling an even number on a number cube. Some equivalences are not obvious to students and thus prompt further exploration to understand "why." As equivalence continues to emerge in the study of different mathematical content areas, it fosters a sense of unity and connectedness in the study of mathematics. Likewise, as students solve problems as diverse as counting the possible combinations of shirts and shorts in a wardrobe and measuring the area of a rectangle, they begin to see and use a similar multiplicative structure in both situations. Their work in developing computational algorithms highlights properties of multiplication that they can model geometrically, reason about, and express in general terms. Thus, multiplicative structures connect ideas from numbers, algebra, and geometry. Equivalence and multiplicative reasoning help students see that mathematics is not a set of isolated topics but rather a web of closely connected ideas (Hiebert & Carpenter, 1992).

Classroom Applications

Ms. Eagleburger has been working with her fourth graders on division. She wishes to see if her students notice the close connections between multiplication and division. For this purpose she poses the following problem to her class:

My friend Sam is moving to Kansas and so he was having a tag sale this weekend to sell things he didn't want to move, and to make some money to use for his new apartment. Just selling his old SEGA games he made $328. If he sold them at $8 apiece, how many do you think he sold?

In this vignette (adapted from Fosnot & Dolk, 2001, pp. 64–70), we listen in as Ms. Eagleburger's class takes up the problem.

"Wow," several students respond as they learn how much her friend Sam made. "What did he charge?" Ms. Eagleburger replies, "Eight dollars apiece. How many did he sell?" "He must have had a lot," says Raj. "That's what I want you to figure out," replies Ms. Eagleburger. "Can we go work on it now?" Gary speaks for the class. "I've got a way to start already!"

The students set off to work in pairs. Several students—using repeated addition—add 8s by doubling until they reach 328. A few students—making tally marks on drawing paper—count in groups of 8s. Others—using the distributive property of multiplication—make use of multiplication facts they know. When all the students have finished their calculations, Ms. Eagleburger calls the class back together for discussion and begins, "Okay Emmanuel, let's start with you." Emmanuel comes to the front and displays a large chart. "I made a chart," he says.

Figure 9.1

llllllll	8
llllllll	16
llllllll	24
llllllll	32
. . . . . .	
llllllll	328

On his chart he has written the multiples of 8—that is, 8, 16, 24, 32, and so on, to 328—as a way of keeping track as he goes along. "Then I counted all the numbers. He sold forty-one SEGA games!" His classmates all agree with his answer.

"Can we share next?" Kathleen asks. "We have a fast way." Kathleen and Miriam bring up their chart and fasten it next to Emmanuel's chart. Miriam begins, "We started to add up eights, but after we wrote down six of them, we realized that we knew six times eight. It's forty-eight. So we wrote that." Kathleen continues, "Then two forty-eights. So that is . . . twelve eights. And we added forty-eight and for tyeight. That's ninety-six. Then we did another forty-eight, and another. We kept going like that until we got to two hundred and eighty-eight. Then to get to three hundred and twenty-eight, we needed to add forty, five more eights."

Figure 9.2

```
48
48  >  96
48
48  >  96
48
48  >  96
40
----
328
```

Ms. Eagleburger looks around the room and asks, "Does anyone have a question for Kathleen and Miriam?" Leah speaks up, "I do. Why did you do six times eight in the first place?" Kathleen and Miriam shrug their shoulders. "I don't know," Kathleen tries to explain. "It just seemed easier.

We knew six times eight." "But adding forty eights is hard," Leah responds. "Why didn't you pick an easier number?" Ms. Eagleburger asks, "Like what, Leah? Do you have a suggestion for Kathleen and Miriam?" Leah brings her chart up on which she has written, "80 + 80 + 80 + 80 = 320." "I did eighties," she explains. "So because I just knew ten times eight was eighty, I knew it was forty-one games." "That's sort of like my way," Jake says. "But I did four times eight first. I knew that was thirty-two. And ten times that is three hundred and twenty."

Both Leah and Jake are using very efficient strategies. Jake's strategy, in a sense, is the basis of the standard division algorithm—that is, at each step he essentially maximizes the trial quotient. However, each of the strategies presented is closely connected with the other: Emmanuel demonstrates that one can partition 328 into 41 groups of 8; Kathleen and Miriam demonstrate that one can partition 328 into (12 + 12 + 12 + 5) groups of 8; Leah demonstrates that one can partition 328 into (10 + 10 + 10 + 10 + 1) groups of 8; and Jake demonstrates that one can partition 328 into (40 + 1) groups of 8. In a subsequent discussion, so as to deepen her students' understanding of the more efficient strategies, Ms. Eagleburger will encourage her students to notice the connections between these strategies—that is, their resemblances and differences.

Precautions and Possible Pitfalls

Although a teacher may be tempted to have all children begin with the most efficient computational strategy—for example, the strategy proposed by Jake—all children do not come into a classroom with the same skills and prior understanding. Children need opportunities to build on their own understandings and opportunities to publicly compare and contrast their strategies and those of their peers. The purpose of any one lesson is not to get all children to the same point, but to explore connections among ideas and solutions (Fosnot & Dolk, 2001). The purpose is to challenge each child and simultaneously develop a "shared sense of the class's base of public knowledge" (Ball & Bass, 2003).

Sources

Ball, D. L., & Bass, H. (2003). Making mathematics reasonable in school. In J. Kilpatrick, W. G. Martin, & D. Shifter (Eds.), *A research companion to Principles and standards for school mathematics*. Reston, VA: NCTM.

Fosnot, C. T., & Dolk, M. (2001). *Young mathematicians at work: Constructing multiplication and division*. Portsmouth, NH: Heinemann.

Hiebert, J., & Carpenter, T. P. (1992). Learning and teaching with understanding. In D. A. Grouws (Ed.), *Handbook of research on mathematics teaching and learning,* pp. 65–97. New York: Macmillan.

NCTM. (2000). *Principles and standards for school mathematics.* Reston, VA: NCTM.

STRATEGY 43: *Select tasks that help students explore and develop increasingly sophisticated mathematical ideas.*

NCTM Standard

What should be the teacher's role in developing connections in Grades 3 through 5?

What Research and the NCTM Standards Say (NCTM, 2000)

Teachers should select tasks that help students explore and develop increasingly sophisticated mathematical ideas. They should ask questions that encourage and challenge students to explain new ideas and develop new strategies based on mathematics they already know. Teachers should encourage students to look for mathematical ideas throughout the school day. Teachers should build on everyday experiences to encourage the study of mathematical ideas through systematic quantitative investigations of situations that students can experience concretely (Hiebert & Carpenter, 1992).

Although the teacher's role includes being alert and responsive to unexpected opportunities during a mathematics lesson, it is also important that teachers plan ahead to integrate mathematics into other subject areas and experiences that students will have during the year. Realistic contexts that can be naturally mathematized are particularly effective in making mathematics a challenging, engaging, and exciting domain of study.

Classroom Applications

Ms. Wilson's fourth grade runs a snack shop for two weeks every school year to pay for a trip to meet the class's pen pals in a neighboring state. Since the students run the whole project, from planning what to sell to recording sales and reordering stock, Ms. Wilson uses this project as an opportunity for students to develop and use mathematical ideas. It is clear that a great deal of estimation and calculation takes place naturally as part of the project: projecting what will be needed for the trip, making change, keeping records of expenses, calculating income, and so forth. This year Ms. Wilson wishes to extend some of the ideas about collecting and describing data that her students had encountered in their work on this project.

In this vignette (adapted from Russell, Schifter, & Bastable, as quoted in NCTM, 2000, p. 204), Ms. Wilson has given the class a list of 21 items, available at a local warehouse club, that she and the principal have approved as possible sale items. She has told the students that they needed to decide which of these products they would sell and how they would allocate the $100 provided for their start-up costs to buy certain quantities of those products. Because the class had limited time to make these decisions, they have engaged in a lively discussion about how best to find out which of the snack items were most popular among the students in the school.

Cindy and Ana insist that they need to survey all classes in order to get "the correct information." If they surveyed only some students, they contended, then "we won't give everyone a chance, so we won't know about something that maybe only one person likes." Others students argue that surveying one or two classes at each grade level would provide enough of an idea of what students across the grades like and would result in a set of data they could collect and organize more efficiently. As they talk, Ms. Wilson reminds her students of the purpose of their survey and asks, "Will our business fail if we don't have everyone's favorite?" The class eventually decides to survey one class at each grade level. Even those students who had worried that a sample would not give them complete information have become convinced that this procedure will give them enough information to make good choices about which snacks to buy.

Over the following week, students design their survey—which raises new issues—and collect, organize, and use the data to develop their budget. Once they have their data, another intense discussion ensues about how to use the information to guide their choices on how to stock their snack shop. The students eventually choose to buy the two top choices in each category (they had classified the snacks into four categories), and since that doesn't use up their budget, they order additional quantities of the overall top two snacks.

Ms. Wilson has used the context of a school store to help her students see how decisions about designing data investigations are tied to the practical problem being addressed. The real restrictions of time and resources challenge her students' thinking about how a sample can be selected to represent a population and about how to interpret this data in light of the stocking decisions they needed to make.

Precautions and Possible Pitfalls

⚠ It is important that children experience the power of mathematics in situations that they might find to be personally relevant. However, teachers should note that although connecting mathematics to the everyday world may increase engagement, it also risks decreasing access. One teacher (Ball, 1995), writing of her third-grade teaching experiences, notes that "using the outside world as a context for my young children's mathematical development at times invited in that world ways that seemed, paradoxically, to deflate the transformative possibilities of our pursuits." Sometimes personal examples created "meanness or disrespect," sometimes "concrete contexts were unevenly familiar or interesting to boys and girls, to international and U.S. children, to children with big families and children with no siblings living with a single parent." Sometimes it was "a little piece of number theory" that fanned the spark of "intellectual excitement."

Sources

Ball, D. L. (1995). Transforming pedagogy: Classrooms as mathematical communities: A response to Timothy Lensmire and John Pryor. *Harvard Educational Review, 65,* 671–677.

Hiebert, J., & Carpenter, T. P. (1992). Learning and teaching with understanding. In D. A. Grouws (Ed.), *Handbook of research on mathematics teaching and learning,* pp. 65–97. New York: Macmillan.

NCTM. (2000). *Principles and standards for school mathematics.* Reston, VA: NCTM.

Russell, S. J., Schifter, D., & Bastable, V. (1999). *Working with data casebook. Pilot-test draft. Developing mathematical ideas.* Newton, MA: Education Development Center.

10

Representation

Grades PreK–2

Young students use many varied representations to build new under-standings and express mathematical ideas. Representing ideas and connecting the representations to mathematics lie at the heart of understanding mathematics. Teachers should analyze students' rep-resentations and carefully listen to their discussions to gain insights into the development of mathematical thinking and to enable them to provide support as students connect their languages to the con-ventional language of mathematics. The goals of the Communication Standard are closely linked with those of this Standard, with each set contributing to and supporting the other.

Students in prekindergarten through Grade 2 represent their thoughts about, and understanding of, mathematical ideas through oral and written language, physical gestures, drawings, and invented and conventional symbols (Edwards, Gandini, & Forman, 1993). These representations are methods for communicating as well as powerful tools for thinking. The process of linking different representations, including technological ones, deepens students' understanding of mathematics because of the connections they make between ideas and the ways the ideas can be expressed. Teachers can gain insight into students' thinking and their grasp of mathematical concepts by exam-ining, questioning, and interpreting their representations. Although a striking aspect of children's mathematical development in the preK–2 years is their growth in using standard mathematical symbols, teachers at this level should encourage students to use multiple representa-tions, and they should assess the level of mathematical understanding conveyed by those representations (NCTM, 2000).

STRATEGY 44: *Encourage young children to represent their mathematical ideas and procedures in varied ways.*

NCTM Standard

What should representation look like in Grades PreK through 2?

What Research and the NCTM Standards Say (NCTM, 2000)

Young students represent their mathematical ideas and proce-dures in many ways. They use physical objects such as their own fingers, natural language, drawings, diagrams, physical gestures, and symbols. Students' representations provide a record of their efforts to understand mathematics and it is through interactions with such representations, other students, and the teacher that students develop their own mental images of mathematical ideas (Smith, 2003).

Classroom Applications

Representations can make mathematical ideas more concrete and more available for further reflection and manipulation. Ms. Brinkerhoff has read Rooster's Off to See the World *(Carle, 1971) to her first-grade class—two cats, then three frogs, four turtles, and five fish join the rooster as he goes off to see the world—and asked them to find out how many, including the rooster, went on the trip. In this vignette (adapted from NCTM, 2000, pp. 137–138), we listen in as several students give their representations and solutions.*

Several students draw the animals and number them. Ashley and Danielle model the animals with counters, count, and write "15" on their papers. Other students used more traditional notations such as tallies, and Gary wrote zero because all the animals had gone home when it got dark. However, Ms. Brinkerhoff was puzzled by Kimberly's answer, which was 21. When Ms. Brinkerhoff asked Kimberly to explain, Kimberly responded that she had noticed while Ms. Brinkerhoff was reading that there were fireflies in the story on the page where the animals decided to turn around and go home. Kimberly wasn't sure how many, but she thought there were six because that was the pattern she had noticed:

Figure 10.1

I	(rooster)
I I	(cats)
I I I	(frogs)
I I I I	(turtles)
I I I I I	(frogs)
I I I I I I	(fireflies)

So she also drew the six fireflies and then, adding the tallies she had made at the top of her paper, got 21.

Problem solving requires that children develop the ability to mathematize situations (Smith, 2003). The problem posed by Ms. Brinkerhoff requires her students to strip away the context of the story and examine its mathematical underpinning. While Ashley and Danielle model the story using familiar representations such as counters, Kimberly and other children use tally marks. Additionally, Kimberly models what she considers to be the mathematical structure of the story. Ms. Brinkerhoff will later ask her students to share their representations, helping them to recognize both the power and the common mathematical nature of different representations.

Precautions and Possible Pitfalls

In mathematics classrooms with a more tradition-oriented focus, young children usually work with abstract and general mathematical representations such as the addition or subtraction algorithms. In mathematics classrooms with a more reform-oriented focus, children are usually encouraged to create and use idiosyncratic representations that "(a) faithfully re-produce the action of a story problem; (b) strip away the content, attending to only the numerical aspects of the problem; or (c) combine some of both approaches" (Smith, 2003). However, it is critical that reform-oriented teachers realize that the goal of such representing is not to replace the standard algorithms (e.g., those of addition or subtraction), but for students to explore problem situations with an eye to developing their computational fluency; in particular, the ability to mathematize.

Sources

Carle, E. (1971). *Rooster's off to see the world*. Natick, MA: Picture Book Studio.

Edwards, C., Gandini, L., and Forman, G. (1993). The hundred languages of children: The Reggio Emilia approach to early childhood education. Norwood, NJ: Ablex Publishing Corp.

NCTM. (2000). *Principles and standards for school mathematics*. Reston, VA: NCTM.

Smith, S. P. (2003). Representation in school mathematics: Children's representations of problems. In J. Kilpatrick, W. G. Martin, & D. Shifter (Eds.), *A research companion to* Principles and standards for school mathematics. Reston, VA: NCTM.

STRATEGY 45: *Create a learning environment that supports and encourages children's use of multiple representations.*

NCTM Standard

What should be the teacher's role in developing representation in Grades PreK through 2?

What Research and the NCTM Standards Say (NCTM, 2000)

A major responsibility of teachers is to create a learning environment in which students' use of multiple representations is encouraged, supported, and accepted by their peers and adults. Teachers should guide students to develop and use multiple representations effectively (Goldin, 2003). Students will thus develop their own perceptions, create their own evidence, structure their own analytical processes, and become confident and competent in their use of mathematics.

Students should be encouraged to share their different representations to help them consider other perspectives and ways of explaining their thinking. Teachers can model conventional ways of representing mathematical situations, but it is important for students to use representations that are meaningful to them. Transitions to conventional notations should be connected to the methods and thinking of the students (NCTM, 2000).

Classroom Applications

After working with his second graders on different ways of mathematizing subtraction problems, Mr. Lawson has modeled for them the conventional pencil-and-paper subtraction algorithm. However, he notices that Corey, one of his students, does not show marks to cross out any digits or write a small "1" to represent "borrowing" that is usual when using this algorithm. That is, Corey writes

Figure 10.2

$$
\begin{array}{r}
74 \\
-28 \\
\hline
46
\end{array}
\quad \text{instead of} \quad
\begin{array}{r}
{}^{6}\!\!\!\not{7}{}^{1}\!\!4 \\
-28 \\
\hline
46
\end{array}
$$

and consistently produces correct answers. In this vignette (adapted from NCTM, 2000, pp. 140–141), we listen in as Mr. Lawson probes.

Corey replies, "My mother showed me another way." Mr. Lawson asks, "Can you show me?" Corey responds, "From eight to fourteen—that is six, and we need to add one to the two (the 2 in the 28) because we used fourteen instead of four." Corey writes 6 in the units place and continues, "From three to seven (the 7 in 74) is four," and he writes 4 in the tens column. Mr. Lawson rephrases the second part of the method, emphasizing the notion of place value. "So, you add ten to the twenty and then subtract thirty from seventy?" Corey nods, "Yes."

Mr. Lawson realizes that Corey's method is based on a property the class has recently discussed: that the same number can be added to both terms of a difference and the result does not change. That is, the difference of 74 – 28 stays the same if one adds 10 to 74 or one adds 10 to 28:

$$74 - 28 = 74 + 10 - (10 + 28)$$

So he invites the class to talk about the process Corey is using. After some discussion, Meghan explains, "You are adding ten to seventy-four because you really did fourteen minus eight:

$$74 + 10 - 8 = 70 + (14 - 8)$$

and you also added ten to twenty-eight because you did seventy minus thirty:

$$74 - 28 = 70 + (14 - 8) - (10 + 20)$$
$$= (14 - 8) + 70 - 30$$

So the answer is the same."

Note how Mr. Lawson both validates Corey's solution and provides opportunities for his class to use multiple representations to look deeper into the properties of subtraction. He does this not to replace the standard subtraction algorithm but to further and expand his students' understanding of the conventional ways of representing the process of subtracting numbers.

Precautions and Possible Pitfalls

The subtraction algorithm Corey has learned—the equal additions algorithm—is still taught in a few locations outside the United States. However, prior to 1821, this algorithm was one of the predominant subtraction algorithms used in the United States (Johnson, 1938). Teachers should note that either this algorithm or the more usual decomposition algorithm is a valid and efficient mathematical tool for subtraction and can be effectively used in developing children's skills with and understanding of subtraction. The equal additions algorithm makes plain that the difference between two numbers remains constant as they are translated along the number line. On the other hand, the conventional decomposition algorithm seems to be better suited to being modeled with manipulatives.

Sources

Goldin, G. (2003). Representation in school mathematics: A unifying research perspective. In J. Kilpatrick, W. G. Martin, & D. Shifter (Eds.), *A research companion to* Principles and standards for school mathematics. Reston, VA: NCTM.

Johnson, J. T. (1938). *The relative merits of three methods of subtraction: An experimental comparison of the decomposition method of subtraction with the equal additions method and the Austrian method.* New York: Bureau of Publications, Teachers College, Columbia University.

NCTM. (2000). *Principles and standards for school mathematics.* Reston, VA: NCTM.

Grades 3–5

In Grades 3–5, students need to develop and use a variety of representations of mathematical ideas to model problem situations, to investigate mathematical relationships, and to justify or disprove conjectures. They should use informal representations, such as drawings, to highlight various features of problems; they should use physical models to represent and understand ideas such as multiplication and place value. They should also learn to use equations, charts, and graphs to model and solve problems. These representations serve as tools for thinking about and solving problems. They also help students communicate their thinking to others. Students in these grades will use both external models—ones that they can build, change, and inspect—as well as mental images (NCTM, 2000).

STRATEGY 46: Encourage students to use representations to support, clarify, and extend their mathematical ideas.

NCTM Standard

What should representation look like in Grades 3 through 5?

What Research and the NCTM Standards Say (NCTM, 2000)

Students in Grades 3–5 should continue to develop the habit of representing problems and ideas to support and extend their reasoning. Such representations can help portray, clarify, or extend a mathematical idea by providing a focus on essential features. Students represent ideas when they create a table of data about weather patterns, when they describe in words or with a picture the important features of an object such as a cylinder, or when they translate aspects of a problem into an equation. Good representations fulfill several roles: they are tools for thinking, tools for problem solving, and instruments for communicating.

Learning to interpret, use, and construct useful representations needs careful and deliberate attention in the classroom. Teaching *forms* of representation (e.g., graphs or equations) as ends in themselves is not productive. Rather, representations should be portrayed as useful tools for solving problems, building understanding, for communicating information, and for demonstrating reasoning (Greeno & Hall, 1997). Students should become flexible in choosing and creating representations—standard or nonstandard, physical models or mental images—that fit the purpose at hand. They should also have many opportunities to consider the advantages and limitations of the various representations they use.

Classroom Applications

Ms. Selnes and her fifth graders have been working on adding and multiplying fractions. Her students have used both symbolic and pictorial representations to mathematize various addition and multiplication strategies. When Lis, one of her students, brings up the idea of having a party and making pizza, Ms. Selnes sees an opportunity for her students to practice what they have been learning. In this vignette (adapted from Fosnot & Dolk, 2002, pp. 66–70), we listen in as Ms. Selnes poses the following problem that she and a colleague, Ms. Cameron, have designed.

> If we make small pan-size pizzas and invite guests, and if we want everyone to have three-fourths of a pan-size pizza, how many pizzas would we need for a given number of people?

Charles raises his hand and asks, "Don't we have to know how many guests?" Ms. Selnes replies, "Yes, when we start making the pizzas. Right now, I need you to figure out ways that we might use when we do know how many people." The children eagerly begin working.

Gary, numbering the people 1, 2, 3, and so on, uses repeated addition and writes:

Figure 10.3

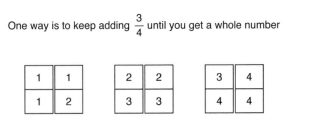

One way is to keep adding $\frac{3}{4}$ until you get a whole number

Four children in the group and three pan-size pizzas

Kimberley draws a diagram similar to the one Gary drew, notices that three pizzas feed four children, and then doubles. She writes:

What you have to do is just double and the doubling goes on forever

6 pizzas	8 kids
12 pizzas	16 kids
24 pizzas	32 kids

Charles and Meghan do not draw a diagram. They treat $\frac{3}{4}$ an operator and write:

4 kids and 3 pan-size pizzas, because if 4 kids get $\frac{3}{4} \times 4 = \frac{12}{4} = 3$

or 18 pizzas and 24 kids, 18 is $\frac{3}{4}$ of 24

or 24 pizzas and 32 kids because 24 is $\frac{3}{4}$ of 32

Lots of possibilities but there has to be a ratio of 3 to 4

$\frac{3}{4}$ y where y = the number of people

The representations that students use are resources for resolving problem situations (Smith, 2003) since students who represent the problem in some way are more likely to see important relationships than those who consider the problem without a representation. The problem that Ms. Selnes has posed for her fifth graders provides opportunities for them to develop, validate, and communicate such resources.

Precautions and Possible Pitfalls

It is known that some (a relatively few) children easily and accurately solve difficult mathematics problems and develop effective and powerful representations without some degree of teacher guidance. However, teachers should not infer that other children (the large majority) are inherently limited in their ability to understand mathematical ideas. What is crucial in development of such abilities are opportunities for children to explore representational modes beyond that of the standard manipulation of formal notational systems—for example, modes of pattern recognition and analogical reasoning (Goldin, 2003)—and the expectations (albeit realistic ones) of their teachers.

Sources

Fosnot, C. T., & Dolk, M. (2002). *Young mathematicians at work: Constructing fractions, decimals, and percents.* Portsmouth, NH: Heinemann.

Goldin, G. (2003). Representation in school mathematics: A unifying research perspective. In J. Kilpatrick, W. G. Martin, & D. Shifter (Eds.), *A research companion to* Principles and standards for school mathematics. Reston, VA: NCTM.

Greeno, J. G., & Hall, R. B. (1997). Practicing representation: Learning with and about representational forms. *Phi Delta Kappan*, pp. 361–367.

NCTM. (2000). *Principles and standards for school mathematics.* Reston, VA: NCTM.

Smith, S. P. (2003). Representation in school mathematics: Children's representations of problems. In J. Kilpatrick, W. G. Martin, & D. Shifter (Eds.), *A research companion to* Principles and standards for school mathematics. Reston, VA: NCTM.

STRATEGY 47: *Choose tasks that embody rich and varied representational structures.*

NCTM Standard

What should be the teacher's role in developing representation in Grades 3 through 5?

What Research and the NCTM Standards Say (NCTM, 2000)

Teachers can choose tasks that students can represent in a meaningful fashion and that embody "rich and varied representational structures, including contextual mathematics, abstract mathematics, and visual imagery" (Goldin, 2003). Teachers should also emphasize the importance of representing mathematical ideas in a variety of ways. Different representations reveal distinctive ways of thinking about a problem, and teachers can, by giving attention to these different insights as well as to the representations, help students see the power of viewing a problem from different perspectives.

By listening carefully to students' ideas and helping them select and organize representations that will show their thinking, teachers can help students develop the inclination and skills to model problems effectively, to clarify their own understanding of a problem, and to use representations to communicate effectively with one another. Observing how different students select and use representations also gives the teacher assessment information about what aspects of the problem they notice and how they reason about the patterns and regularities revealed in their representations.

Classroom Applications

In order to better plan the next few weeks of classwork, Mr. Bratton wants to gain a deeper understanding of his fifth graders' communication and problem-solving skills. What he thinks would be most useful is the creation of a learning experience that would provide opportunities for his students to design and discuss a variety of representational strategies. While reading through an old copy of Teaching Children Mathematics, *he comes across the following task (Ferrini-Mundy, Lappan, & Phillips, 1997):*

Tat Ming is designing square swimming pools. Each pool has a square center that is the area of the water. Tat Ming uses black tiles to represent the water. Around each pool there is a border of white tiles. Here are pictures of the three smallest square pools that he can design with black tiles for the interior and white tiles for the border.

Figure 10.4

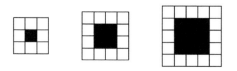

1. Make a table showing the area of the pool and white tiles for the border for the first six square pools.

2. Find the number of white tiles in the 10th pool. The 25th pool. The 100th pool.

For his purposes and his class, this seems ideal. In this vignette (adapted from Ferrini-Mundy, Lappan, & Phillips, 1997), we listen in as Mr. Bratton walks around the room talking to and listening to his students as they work on the task.

Most of the students have completed the following table:

Pool Number	White Tiles	Area
1	8	9
2	12	16
3	16	25
4	20	36
5	24	49
6	28	64

However, Gary has noted, while looking at the squares rather than the table, that the border—the white tiles—"goes up by fours." Mr. Bratton asks him why and Gary replies, "This is one (pointing to the black square in the first pool). It only has one white square on each side. This has two (pointing to the side of the black square in the second pool). So it multiplies, I mean, goes up by four, because you add a white one to each side" (he shades in the ones added).

Figure 10.5

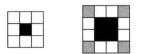

He continues, "So the number of white tiles in the tenth pool would be forty-four?" Mr. Bratton smiles and says, "Does that match what you see in your table?"

Mr. Bratton walks over to where Rebecca is working. She looks up and says, "Look, I've found a pattern. The area of the first pool is nine and the area of the third pool is twenty-five and the difference is sixteen."

Pool Number	White Tiles	Area
1	8	9
2	12	16
3	25 − 9 = 16	25
4	36 − 16 = 20	36
5	24	49
6	28	64

Mr. Bratton looks puzzled. Rebecca continues, "If I subtract the area of the first pool from the area of the third pool, I get the number of white tiles in the third pool." Mr. Bratton says, "What about the other pools?" Rebecca smiles and says, "The fourth pool is thirty-six, and thirty-six minus sixteen, the area of the second pool, is twenty. That's the number of tiles in the fourth pool!" Mr. Bratton asks, "Why do you think that works?" Rebecca looks unsure. Mr. Bratton continues, "How about the pool pictures?" Rebecca looks at the pictures of the pools for a moment and says, "Oh, I see. The first pool fits inside the third pool. So the difference is the border."

Figure 10.6

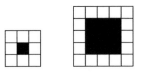

Mr. Bratton smiles and replies, "Does that always work?"

Note how this task gives rise to various representations. As Mr. Bratton questions other students, he finds that Ryan, while looking at the sides of each pool, has noticed that the number of white tiles is 4 times one more than the pool number. That is,

$$\text{White tiles} = 4 \times (\text{Pool Number} + 1)$$

Note also how Mr. Bratton encourages his students to question and clarify their present representation in the light of other possible representations. Such moving among representations encourages students to expand their problem-solving repertoires and deepen their understandings of the structure of the mathematics.

Precautions and Possible Pitfalls

Good representations provide varied ways of unpacking a mathematics problem. However, it is essential that teachers realize that, in this sense, there are no *perfect* representations, but, at best, representations that generally take into account particular content and a particular child's mathematical abilities and mathematical interests. What is critical is that teachers both understand and are able to reconcile the mathematics behind the representations they encourage and support, and that they have alternative models in reserve to compensate for the imperfections and distortions in any given representation (Ball, 1993).

Sources

Ball, D. L. (1993). With an eye on the mathematical horizon: Dilemmas of teaching elementary school mathematics. *The Elementary School Journal, 93,* 172–197.

Ferrini-Mundy, J., Lappan, G., & Phillips, E. (1997). Experiences with patterning. *Teaching Children Mathematics, 3,* 282–288.

Goldin, G. (2003). Representation in school mathematics: A unifying research perspective. In J. Kilpatrick, W. G. Martin, & D. Shifter (Eds.), *A research companion to* Principles and standards for school mathematics. Reston, VA: NCTM.

NCTM. (2000). *Principles and standards for school mathematics.* Reston, VA: NCTM.

Epilogue

We hope that you have found this book both informative and useful. We caution that while the vignettes do tell stories of actual teachers and actual students doing mathematics, they are not blueprints for a lesson. The vignettes, the suggested research-based strategies, and the supporting discussion were intended to indicate ways in which a teacher might implement many of the teaching practices and learning experiences recommended by the NCTM. If you wish to design, plan, or implement comparable lessons, many of the references quoted provide the essential and necessary details.

Children in Grades PreK–5 are often enthusiastic about learning and doing mathematics—approximately three-quarters of American fourth graders say they like mathematics.[1] Such interest and enthusiasm can make teaching in these grades exciting and challenging. However, these statistics should also be sobering, as it appears that this enthusiasm has significantly waned by middle school, and this lack of interest and enthusiasm follows many school children into their adult years. Such adults more often than not take pride in their inability to have mastered school mathematics. Furthermore, when they are told that their own children will need to master mathematics in school, they begin to question the reasons for such claims, especially when their children come home with math homework that looks unfamiliar to their parents. Over the years, we have tried to convince others that there is power and beauty in mathematics. This is no easy task. We are often confronted with responses like, "I don't need to know arithmetic since I use the [ubiquitous] calculator." Or, "I don't even have to calculate the 'best buy' in the supermarket, since every item has its unit price indicated." Or "Even 'miles per gallon' need not be calculated, since my car's odometer does that for me." Some even ask, "Why teach mathematics at all?" Why don't they ever ask, "Why teach poetry, literature, music, art, or even science if one is not planning to pursue a career in those fields? When was the last time an adult needed to use any of these subjects in everyday life?"

We need to convince the general populace of the importance of mathematics. Learning mathematics is much more than just obtaining a tool to use in another field. It is the subconscious acquisition of thinking and reasoning skills coupled with the more sophisticated way we view the physical world that leads the list of the many life enhancements that come with learning mathematics. However, simply saying, as many do, that today's students are involved with real-world applications in the classroom just doesn't cut it. Unfortunately, there are at least two problems with the real-world-math claims: First, the real world of students is often not what teachers have chosen to be the real world, and to be truly of the real world—rather than an artificial model—is generally far too complicated for a school audience. There are times when parents do a "project" at home that involves mathematics or reasoning skills. Often these skills were developed as a result of school mathematics instruction. Parents should involve their children in these projects, which might include setting up a birthday party, buying flooring or carpeting, or calculating expenses (i.e., budget). These would be actual real-world activities.

Note

1. Silver, E. A., Strutchens, M. E., & Zawojewski, J. S. (1997). NAEP findings regarding race/ethnicity and gender: Affective issues, mathematics performance, and instructional context. In P. A. Kenney & E. A. Silver (Eds.), *Results from the Sixth Mathematics Assessment of the National Assessment of Educational Progress* (pp. 33–59). Reston, VA: National Council of Teachers of Mathematics.

Index